THE NUYORICAN
EXPERIENCE

THE NUYORICAN EXPERIENCE

Literature of the Puerto Rican Minority

EUGENE V. MOHR

Contributions in American Studies, Number 62

Greenwood Press
Westport, Connecticut · London, England

Library of Congress Cataloging in Publication Data

Mohr, Eugene V.
The Nuyorican experience.

(Contributions in American studies, ISSN 0084-9227 ;
no. 62)
Bibliography: p.
Includes index.
1. American literature—Puerto Rican authors—His-
tory and criticism. 2. American literature—New York
(N.Y.)—History and criticism. 3. American literature—
20th century—History and criticism. 4. Puerto Ricans—
New York (N.Y.)—History. I. Title. II. Series.
PS153.P83M6   1982   810'.9'867295   82-9282
ISBN 0-313-23334-9 (lib. bdg.)   AACR2

Library of Congress Catalog Card Number: 82-9282
ISBN: 0-313-23334-9
ISSN: 0084-9227

First published in 1982

Greenwood Press
A division of Congressional Information Service, Inc.
88 Post Road West
Westport, Connecticut 06881

Printed in the United States of America

10 9 8 7 6 5 4 3 2 1

To my mother
who raised me in New York
and my wife
who migrated me to Puerto Rico

CONTENTS

ACKNOWLEDGMENTS

I am pleased to express my gratitude to the University of Puerto Rico for granting me a sabbatical leave to write this book and to the publishers who granted me permission to quote the materials listed below.

Excerpts from *Short Eyes* by Miguel Piñero. Copyright © 1974, 1975 by Miguel Piñero. Reprinted by permission of Hill and Wang, a division of Ferrar, Straus and Giroux, Inc.

Lines from "Kill, Kill, Kill," "This Is Not the Place Where I Was Born," "A Lower East Side Poem," and "Jitterbug Jesus" in *La Bodega Sold Dreams* by Miguel Piñero. Copyright © 1980 by Arte Público Press. Reprinted by permission of Arte Público Press.

Excerpts from *The Sun Always Shines for the Cool* by Miguel Piñero, in *Revista Chicano-Riqueña* 7, no. 1: 173-204. Copyright © 1979 by *Revista Chicano-Requeña*. Reprinted by permission of *Revista Chicano-Riqueña*.

Excerpts from *Memorias de Bernardo Vega* edited by César Andreu Iglesias. Copyright © 1977 by Ediciones Huracán, Inc. Reprinted by permission of Ediciones Huracán, Inc.

Excerpts from *Down These Mean Streets* by Piri Thomas. Copyright © 1967 by Piri Thomas. Reprinted by permission of Alfred A. Knopf, Inc.

Lines from "under me sometime. under me. walls & paint. 1967" from *Snaps* by Victor Hernandez Cruz. Copyright © 1968, 1969 by Victor Hernandez Cruz. Reprinted by permission of Random House, Inc.

Lines from "The Broken English Dream," "Monday Morning," "O/D," "Puerto Rican Obituary," "Tata," "Poetry," and "Suicide Note from a Cockroach in a Low Income Housing Project" in *Puerto Rican Obituary* by Pedro Pietri. Copyright © 1973 by Pedro Pietri. Reprinted by permission of Monthly Review Press.

Lines from "my graduation speech," "the africa in pedro morejón," and "the salsa of bethesda fountain" in *La Carreta Made a U-Turn* by Tato Laviera. Copyright © 1979 by Arte Público Press. Reprinted by permission of Arte Público Press.

Lines from "El Capitán San Miguelito, *Part Two*" and "Mongo Affair" in *Mongo Affair* by Miguel Algarín. Copyright © 1978 by Miguel Algarín. Reprinted by permission of Arte Público Press.

Lines from "Je me souviens" and "Taos Pueblo Indians: 700 strong according to Bobby's last census" in *On Call* by Miguel Algarín. Copyright © 1980 by Arte Público Press. Reprinted by permission of Arte Público Press.

From *Nuyorican Poetry* edited by Miguel Algarín and Miguel Piñero. Copyright © 1975 by Miguel Algarín and Miguel Piñero. By permission of William Morrow & Company: lines from
  "Counterfeit Quarters" and "Twice a Month Is Mother's Day." Copyright © 1975 by Miguel Piñero.
  "The Sounds of Sixth Street." Copyright © 1975 by Martita Morales.
  "San Juan/ an arrest/ Maguayo/ a vision of Malo dancing" and "Inside Control: my tongue." Copyright © 1975 by Miguel Algarín.
  And excerpts from Algarín's prose commentary.

Some of the references in this study are to widely distributed reprint editions and are identified as such. Nicholasa Mohr's *Nilda* and *El Bronx Remembered* were originally published by Harper & Row, Inc. Her *In Nueva York* was originally published by The Dial Press. Piri Thomas's *Down These Mean Streets* was originally published by Alfred A. Knopf, Inc.

Chapter 4 of this study is a revision of an article which appeared in *Revista Chicano-Riqueña* 8, no. 4 (1980): 60-68.

INTRODUCTION

Although Puerto Ricans have had a colony in New York for well over a century, their presence as a large, unassimilated mass in the melting pot became suddenly obvious around the time of World War II. And by the early 1950s *El Mundo*, San Juan's leading Spanish-language newspaper, was referring to New York simply as *la urbe*, the metropolis, exactly the way people all over the Empire referred to Rome in its heyday. Just as London was the metropolitan center for people from Jamaica and Trinidad, Paris for those from Martinique and Guadeloupe, Amsterdam for Surinamese and Curaçaoans, so New York, during the great Caribbean exodus following the war, became the metropolitan center and migration goal for Puerto Ricans of all kinds, but especially for the very poor.

People from everywhere in the Caribbean flowed into New York in greater numbers, in fact, than into any other city in the world.[1] But the Puerto Ricans have been the most conspicuous: they started earlier and migrated on a more massive scale than any other group; furthermore, as legal immigrants they did not have to hide, and as American citizens they could apply for all sorts of government services. As a result much more was learned about them than about the others. Puerto Ricans are probably the most studied, researched, card-catalogued, and cross-indexed immigrants in history. The official data about them are not encouraging. Among the nation's ethnic groups they are distinguished by a long list of negatives: lowest family incomes; highest percentage of low-level jobs and of homes without breadwinners; and highest rate of school dropouts and of deaths from homicides, accidents, drug abuse, and cirrhosis of the liver.[2] As statistics Puerto Ricans don't come across very well; most of their fellow Americans, unfortunately, know them only as statistics or as an alien tumor of poverty, terrorism, and crime.

A quite different picture develops in the novels, stories, poetry, and drama in which Puerto Ricans themselves have described several generations of immigrant experience. This personal, largely autobiographical literature is the subject of the present study. It is a literature of both human and social interest, an essential complement to the sociological examinations written, for the most part, by persons whose values and attitudes distance them from the people they write about. Distance is necessary for some types of understanding, but other types require the viewpoint of experience.

The literature of the Puerto Rican immigration is interesting for a variety of reasons and in a variety of contexts. In terms of its size and generational span, it is one of America's richest immigrant literatures. The experiences it describes are similar to those described in the past by Jews, Irish, and Italians, who came seeking a better life in America's cities. There are also differences in the Puerto Rican experience, differences due partly to changed times and attitudes, partly to the special relationships— political, economic, and geographic—between Puerto Rico and the United States. Another aspect of Puerto Rican immigrant writing is its relationship to contemporary ethnic literatures, like those of blacks and Chicanos, which question the traditional insistence on "Americanization" and often express anger in place of hope or gratitude. The dual nature—immigrant and ethnic— of the Puerto Rican writing reflects the fact that it covers a long period of time and includes the different reactions of first, second, and even third generations. This chronological ordering is the basis of the chapter divisions that follow.

The first chapter, for example, discusses autobiographical works by three Puerto Ricans who migrated to New York around 1920 and spent most of their lives on the mainland. Although they all mention the city's Puerto Rican population, it is not the population that later coalesced into isolated communities in Spanish Harlem, the South Bronx, and the Lower East Side. A strong sense of the ghetto, particularly El Barrio, first appears in books dealing with the hundreds of thousands of poor and functionally illiterate migrants who flooded the city during World War II and the following decade. These people did not have the tools to write about themselves; their story was told by Island writers who visited the New York colony and sometimes projected their own cultural concerns on men and women whose main preoccupation was simply staying alive. These books, discussed in chapter 2, were written in Spanish by established authors and directed at Island readers.

Chapters 3 to 5 discuss works written in English by second-generation Puerto Ricans—those whose parents had migrated—or by those who migrated as children and were formed by the city. Their experiences are similar to those recorded by the children of earlier immigrants: Michael Gold's *Jews Without Money* is an obvious parallel to works by writers like Piri Thomas and Nicholasa Mohr (no connection with the present writer). Typically in this literature there is conflict between the child's desire to blend in with the American world outside and his need for the love and attention of his "foreign" parents. Then, to mediate these conflicts, there are street gangs—logical adaptations of our westerns and gangster films—little "American" societies where the poor and the accented and the miscolored can belong. The threat of crime born of poverty and social rejection is a common element. So are the immigrant's ambiguous feelings toward what he regards as specifically American institutions—public schools and welfare agencies, for example—and toward his ghetto or *barrio*, a symbol of both acceptance and alienation.

The final chapters deal with a group of younger writers, mostly poets and playwrights in their thirties, who have been touched by broader social currents and who point out possible new directions for the literature and the community. Assimilation into mainstream culture is one such possibility, though constricted by the individual's racial makeup. There is also considerable interest in the creation of a totally new lifestyle out of a multitude of bits and patches of influence: ethnic and linguistic background, music, street codes, drugs, television and movies, the neighborhood. Then there is the possibility of returning to Puerto

Rico, an increasingly common phenomenon in real life, but as yet only touched upon in literature.

This study is not a history of the literature arising from the Puerto Rican immigration; it does not pretend to the sort of completeness appropriate to that type of work. For one thing, it is concerned only with books about New York, which is home for about half of the 2 million mainland Puerto Ricans.[3] New York really represents the United States for Puerto Ricans. In the first decade or two of the great migration those of limited education used *Nova Yor* or *los Novayores* to refer to any part of the country. This usage has pretty well died out, but New York remains *la urbe*, basic symbol of the American adventure. In any case, very little writing has emerged from Puerto Rican communities elsewhere on the mainland. New York is, moveover, the metropolis of nearly all our immigrant literatures.

It will become necessary below to distinguish Spanish-speaking immigrants, born and raised on the Island, from their English-speaking children molded in New York. Various terms, such as "Nuyorican" and "Neorican," are used to refer to the English speakers, particularly to distinguish them from the "real" Puerto Ricans who never lived away from the Island. The use of such terms is resented by some, especially those who eventually return to Puerto Rico: it's hard, in one lifetime, to be a *spic* in New York and then a *Nuyorriqueño* back home. In New York, on the other hand, the need for some such term is increasingly recognized, and poets like Miguel Algarín and Miguel Piñero call themselves Nuyoricans with feelings of dignity and pride. This is as it should be. They have struggled against difficult obstacles; from poverty and social oppression they have refashioned themselves into dynamic bilingual, bicultural people with a cultural definition all their own. It is with these positive connotations that the word Nuyorican is used in this book.

A word must be said about the norms of selection and criticism followed here. Literary merit is the basic principle of selection but always within the boundaries of the proposed subject matter. The authors discussed, with the exception of a few references, are either Puerto Ricans who have lived in New York or persons born in New York of Puerto Rican parents. Books are mentioned only if they relate to the migratory experience. The extensive sociological literature on this subject is not part of the present study, though many of its findings are tacitly assumed throughout. The bibliography includes, in addition to works referred to in the text, titles of relevant sociological studies and of works excluded from discussion either because they have small literary interest or because their inclusion would have made the discussion repetitious.

NOTES

1. For information on this movement, see the special issue on Caribbean migration to New York of *International Migration Review* 13, no. 2 (1979).
2. "El ascenso de los hispanos," *El Nuevo Día* [San Juan, P.R.], 30 August 1981, p. 38.
3. Samuel-René Quiñones, "Migration to U.S. of Puerto Ricans has altered island," *San Juan Star*, 9 August 1981, p. 1.

THE NUYORICAN
EXPERIENCE

1

PROTO-NUYORICANS

The best firsthand sources of information about New York's Puerto Rican community before World War II are three little known autobiographies whose importance lies in adding new material to our knowledge of that period and in describing for the first time the most widespread patterns of Hispanic migration northward. *Memorias de Bernardo Vega* covers, with the aid of a flashback device, the period between the American Civil War and 1947. Jesus Colon's *A Puerto Rican in New York and Other Sketches* refers almost entirely to the period between World Wars I and II. Both Vega and Colon are primarily chroniclers drawing from their unfamiliar data a generally unrecognized image of their fellow Puerto Ricans as hardworking people with a strong political consciousness and a deep commitment to freedom and social justice. In contrast, Pedro Juan Labarthe's *The Son of Two Nations: The Private Life of a Columbia Student* subordinates communal concerns to the Horatio Alger-like efforts of an ambitious young man to win success by exploiting the resources available to him in the wealthier of his two nations.

Bernardo Vega, author of the most interesting of these three books, was a cigarmaker and active trade unionist, friend and companion of labor leader Santiago Iglesias and representative at the constituent assembly of the Puerto Rican Socialist party held at the town of Cayey in 1915. His lifelong association with socialist and communist movements reflected his passion for improving the lot of workers. This and his belief in independence for Puerto Rico were the two guiding principles of his thought and action. In this he was in the vanguard: socialism, enhanced by the imposing presence of Castro's Cuba, has now become an essential component of every movement toward Puerto Rican independence.

In 1916 at the age of thirty, Vega migrated to New York, where for more than thirty years he participated in the lives of his compatriots as laborer, journalist, businessman, and political activist. After he returned to Puerto Rico, he remained active in politics until the day of his death in 1965. His final allegiance was to the Pro-Independence Movement, predecessor of today's Puerto Rican Socialist party. He ended where he began.

The final style and arrangement of the *Memorias* are the work of editor César Andreu Iglesias, a Puerto Rican novelist who—like José Luis González, contributor of a brilliant introductory essay—shared Vega's economic and political creeds. The contents and basic design of the book are Vega's. Information on the years after 1916 is given in the first person; for the period before 1916 the author makes use of a fictional informant named Tío Antonio, who supposedly arrived in New York in 1847 and who conveniently dies in 1918, when Vega has been around long enough to be his own observer. The information given through Tío Antonio was derived from contact with older residents and from painstaking research in public libraries and in Vega's own large collection of books and documents on Puerto Rico and its New York colony. The use of a personal vehicle through which to present this researched material is particularly effective for the exciting years between the American Civil War and the Spanish American War, when New York was the center of the Antillean Independence Movement inspired by resistence to Spain's economic and social oppression and by the hemispheric quest for self-government. The events of those years—mutually suspect negotiations between Spain and the colonies, alliances formed and broken, inter- and intraparty rivalries, repeatedly frustrated attempts to invade Cuba—and the great figures steering those events—Segundo Ruiz Belvis, Ramón Emeterio Betances, Eugenio María de Hostos, Máximo Gómez, José Martí—are pictured with the immediacy of an eyewitness description.

Vega's memoirs are, in aim and content, close to the spirit of an epic. They create the story of a people, New York's Puerto

Ricans, in their historic struggles toward social and political betterment. The heroes are the men and women who played major roles in those struggles, while the community fabric is woven, as in the classic epics, from continual listings—of organizations, meetings, names, figures:

Para este tiempo se fundó la Liga de Artesanos con propósitos culturales y cívicos. Con esta agrupación colaboraron Antonio Molina, Juan de Dios Núñez, Flor Baerga, Jesús Picón y Sotero Figueroa.

Se estableció tambien otra asociación similar, pero integrada por mujeres, con el nombre de Liga Antillana. Se trataba de cubanas y puertorriqueñas pertenecientes a la clase obrera, entre otras Gertrudis E. de Serra, Josefa González, Dominga Muriel, Romona Gomero y Pilar Pivalot.

Around that time the Craftsmen's Association was founded for civic and cultural ends. Antonio Molina, Juan de Dios Núñez, Flor Baerga, Jesús Picón and Sotero Figueroa were active in this group.

Another, similar group was established, this one made up of women, under the name of the Antillean League. It was for Cuban and Puerto Rican women who belonged to the working class and included, among others, Gertrudis E. de Serra, Josefa González, Dominga Muriel, Ramona Gomero and Pilar Pivalot.[1]

Constantly updated statistics are given on the number of Puerto Ricans and other Hispanics in the city, the neighborhoods they occupy, their jobs, businesses, clubs, meetings, and celebrations. Vega is conscientious about his data, sometimes comparing two or three sources:

Sin embargo, recuerdo que para ese tiempo [1927] la New York Mission Society calculaba que in Nueva York residían 150,000 puertorriqueños. El *New York Times*, por su parte, elevaba la cifra a 200,000. En cuanto al total de electores inscriptos, creao que el informe de la Brotherhood se queda corto.

However, I remember that around that time [1927] the New York Mission Society estimated that there were 150,000 Puerto Ricans,

living in New York, while the New York Times *raised the
figure to 200,000. As to the total number of registered voters,
I think that the figure given in the Brotherhood's report is too
low.*[2]

Despite the long lists of specifics and the long time period
covered, *Memorias de Bernardo Vega* is a very homogeneous work,
mostly because of the persistence of its basic themes. When
Vega goes to a Christmas party with old friends in 1939, he sums
up, in describing their conversation, their concerns of the previous fifty years:

> La conversación giró sobre los mismos temas de medio
> siglo antes.
> Hablamos de la lucha de los sindicatos, del problema de
> los viviendas, de los prejuicios raciales, des socialismo, del
> anarchismo, del régimen colonial en Puerto Rico....
> *The conversation turned on the same themes as half a century
> before.*
> *We spoke about the struggle of the unions, the housing prob-
> lem, racial prejudices, socialism, anarchism, the colonial regime
> in Puerto Rico....*[3]

This book deals, then, essentially with ideas, and Vega manages
to build a lot of drama into ideological conflicts and incompatibilities.

The most pervasive conflict, that of Puerto Rican status, is an
issue with an unexpectedly long past. As early as 1869 the movement to throw off the yoke of Spain was split between annexation and independence: "Hostos se percató de la sorda división
entre los partidarios consecuentes de la independencia y los que
aspiraban a la anexión de las islas a Estados Unidos" [*Hostos
became aware of the silent division between those who favored independence and those who hoped the islands would be annexed to the United
States*].[4] In 1898, when the *Maine* was sunk and Cuba was on the
threshold of independence, it was Julio J. Henna, head of the
Puerto Rican section of the Cuban Revolutionary party, who
urged the United States occupation of Puerto Rico. Vega notes
with sad irony that among those Henna negotiated with was
General Miles, "el mismo que habría de dirigir el desembarco de
las tropas en Guánica el 25 de julio de 1898" [*the man who was*

to direct the landing of the troops at Guánica on July 25, 1898].[5] Nevertheless, when Henna, in 1902, persuaded a congressman to introduce a bill granting United States citizenship to Puerto Ricans, the bill was never even discussed in committee. Eventually citizenship was granted, by the Jones Act of 1917, but this did not change the determination of those who favored independence. In fact, about three hundred "men without a country" rejected the proffered citizenship. But most Puerto Ricans agreed with Santiago Iglesias that United States citizenship was a useful base from which to support either statehood, independence, or the "free associated state" defended by Antonio R. Barceló in 1922. Iglesias opposed Barceló's formula as being "ni estado, ni libre ni asociado" [*neither state, nor free, nor associated*],[6] a phrase that was repopularized when Luis Muñoz Marín had a similar status implemented thirty years later.

Vega's commitment to Puerto Rican independence is matched by his dedication to the improvement of the working class and his pride in being a cigarmaker and a union man. The cigarmakers, during the epoch of hand-rolled cigars, considered themselves the intellectuals of the working class because they had won the fringe benefit of having another employee read to them while they worked. The readings at most factories included some of the most advanced social and economic thought of the day and made the listeners keenly aware of their rights and expectations. This awareness, with the consequent demands for better salaries and working conditions, may have hastened the practical disappearance of this class of workers with the advent of machine-made cigars. Vega's inside description of the cigar industry, from its heyday through its demise, is a small but significant contribution to the history of American labor. Not the least interesting aspect of that history is the role Hispanics played in it.

Patriotism and class consciousness are in a recurrent tug-of-war throughout the *Memorias.* Vega would have been a happy man indeed if he had found all Puerto Ricans, in New York and on the Island, espousers of independence and champions of the working class. One senses in his writing a sort of pained bafflement when he has to deal with seemingly good people, especially compatriots, who fail in one or the other of his ideals. He draws a sharp distinction between the working classes on the one hand and the professional, intellectual, and monied classes on the other, with patriotism and social justice the clear prerogatives of the workers. It was the workers who supported the Antillean revolutionary movement in the nineteenth century and the movement toward social justice in the twentieth, while Puerto Rican intellectuals turned their backs upon the workers and Puerto Rican capitalists took money from their native soil and invested it in Florida.[7]

Different ideas about the class struggle also drove a temporary wedge between communists and members of the Puerto Rican Nationalist party, both supporters of independence, over the Nationalists' belief that "implicarse en luchas sociales era desviar a los puertorriqueños de su primordial deber patriótico" [*involvement in social struggles was deflecting Puerto Ricans from their primordial patriotic duty*].[8] The inevitable tension between the two groups often erupted in street fights, and in one of these a young Nationalist was killed.[9] Nevertheless, when the leaders of the Nationalist party were jailed in 1936 for "lucha abierta contra el régimen colonial" [*open conflict with the colonial regime*], the Communist party and other workers' groups united to demand "la libertad inmediata de los presos políticos" [*immediate release of the political prisoners*].[10]

The same bipolarity of idealism complicates Vega's attitudes toward insular politicians, who are measured by the twin yardsticks of liberalism and independence. Muñoz Marín, for all his admitted greatness, is tested like anyone else: praised for his support of labor and for his idealistic leadership of the common man, he is criticized for not supporting the Tydings bill for Puerto Rican independence in 1943.[11]

North Americans and North American institutions are judged mostly on the basis of their social philosophy, and the judgments are often favorable. Vega applauds, for example, the benefits that United States hegemony brought to the Puerto Rican labor movement. These became evident in 1902, when Santiago Iglesias and other labor leaders were sentenced to prison by a Puerto Rican court for conspiring to raise workers' salaries, a crime under Spanish rule. American labor, led by Samuel Gompers, demanded federal intervention. The case was brought before a United States appeals court, which reversed the lower court's decision and thereby established the right of Puerto Rican workers to organize and strike.

Gompers appears many times in this book as a champion of Puerto Rican workers. Largely through his efforts the labor movement in Puerto Rico was drawn into the orbit of United States trade unionism, where it received help and encouragement. In sad contrast, and despite the enlightened attitudes of Gompers and others, some mainland unions barred Puerto Ricans from membership: "Por otra parte, los carpinteros, albañiles, sastres y barberos no eran admitidos como miembros por las uniones de la AFL" [*On the other hand, carpenters, masons, tailors, and barbers were not accepted as members of AFL unions*].[12] This and other obvious cases of discrimination were—and are—due in part to the racial mixture of so many Puerto Ricans and to the refusal of white Puerto Ricans, like Vega, to play the race game by avoiding their darker-skinned fellows. Vega is obviously proud of the example of racial tolerance that working-class Puerto Ricans introduced to the United States:

> No existía separación notable de color entre los nucleos poblacionales puertorriqueños. Especialmente en el sector de las calles 99 y 106 vivían no pocos paisanos negros. . . . En los vecendarios puertorriqueños, como regla general, se vivía en armonía, sin tomarse en cuenta las diferencias raciales.
>
> *No division on the basis of color was noticeable in the Puerto Rican population centers. There were quite a few black Puerto Ricans, especially in the section between 99 and 106 Streets. . . . In the Puerto Rican neighborhoods, as a general rule, people lived harmoniously, without taking racial differences into account.*[13]

One of the names Vega mentions with greatest respect is that of Arturo Alfonso Shomburgh, who was born near San Juan, emigrated to New York, and became one of the outstanding intellectual leaders of the black American community of his day, "¡magnífico ejemplo de identidad de pueblos oprimidos!" [*a magnificent example of the oneness of oppressed people!*][14] Although Shomburgh's "magnificent example" has not cleared away the confusing questions of social identity faced by Hispanics struggling in the swamp of prejudice in the United States, it does serve as an ideal, a reminder that ethnic and racial barriers are not impassible.

More common than acts of specifically racial discrimination in Vega's work are reports of negative, hostile attitudes directed at Puerto Ricans as a cultural subgroup. These attitudes appeared soon after the turn of the century, increased with every expansion of the Hispanic population, and have remained, despite Puerto Rico Day parades, part of the texture of New York life. Vega's approach to anti-Puerto Rican sentiment is not angry or simplistic. He recognizes different reasons for it, one of which is the lazy ignorance that feeds on generalities: "Para la generalidid de los yanquis, los boricuas eran *material gastable*, individuos sin cultura, ignorantes y, por añadidura, carentes de madurez.... ¡Asi nos juzgan muchos todavia!" [*For the average Yankee Puerto Ricans were expendable stuff, individuals without culture, ignorant and immature. . .Many still judge us that way!*][15]

Not all prejudice is so arbitrary, however. Vega deplores those Puerto Ricans who mutilate the tranquility of towns and neighborhoods "con sus alborotos infantiles y su descuido—tirando latas vacias de cerveza por las calles—, lo que nos gana mucha mala voluntad" [*with their infantile noise and carelessness—like tossing empty beer cans in the street—which brings us a lot of bad feeling*].[16] He recognizes that the parties given by Puerto Ricans "irritaban a los vecinos de otras nacionalidades debido a la algazara que formaban" [*annoyed neighbors of other nationalities with the uproar they produced*].[17] As in other such instances, he is quick to add that nothing like that went on in the homes of the cigarmakers, but the cigarmakers suffered from the community image like everyone else.

Puerto Ricans have suffered not only badly but also unjustly for this type of prejudice by membership or association because of the widespread use of fake Puerto Rican birth certificates by criminals and other undesirables from other South and Central American nations. Most of these illegal immigrants settle in New York and blend easily into the "Puerto Rican" community.[18] In the years since Vega lived there, the number of non-Puerto Rican Hispanic immigrants has grown so large that some observers see the possibility that specifically Puerto Rican identity may be lost through merger in an all-embracing Hispanic community.[19]

For Vega the most pernicious source of negative attitudes toward mainland Puerto Ricans has been journalistic exploitation of popular prejudice, a problem from the earliest years of annexation. In 1902 the New York *Morning Sun* described Puerto Ricans as "aborígenes cuyos arcos y flechas han sido sustituidos por revolveres y cuchillos" [*aborigines whose bows and arrows have been replaced by knives and revolvers*], and in 1904 the *Globe* pontificated that Puerto Ricans were not capable of self-government because they had not, as a people, reached maturity.[20]

As the city's Latin population grew, attention shifted from the island to the immigrants themselves. In 1940 *Scribner's Commentator* carried an article titled "Welcome Paupers and Crime: Puerto Rico's shocking gift to U.S.," picturing the Puerto Rican community on the mainland as a morass of welfare dependence, tuberculosis, syphilis, malaria, prostitution, and moral degradation.[21] In 1947, with migration growing, the *World Telegram* published a series of articles so defamatory—Vega quotes from them on pages 278-79—that they caused consternation in Puerto Rico no less than in El Barrio and led to the picketing of the newspaper offices by over a thousand people, including congressman Vito Marcantonio and Communist party leader Ben Davis. Public protests of that sort have helped greatly to moderate anti-minority campaigns in the media and to lessen discrimination in government and private institutions.

Marcantonio, Davis, and liberals like Smith, LaGuardia, and Roosevelt are mentioned frequently, with warm praise. For *Memorias de Bernardo Vega* does not treat the Puerto Rican community as a ghetto isolated from the surrounding city and nation but as warp and woof in the whole cloth of American history. The Great Depression suffered by Hispanics—alleviated a bit by bathroom rum, *la bolita*, flowerpot marihuana, spiritism, and neighborhood beauty contests—is the same Great Depression millions of other New Yorkers are facing in similar ways at the same time. American intervention in Nicaragua and the trial of Sacco and Vanzetti cry out to the nation. And World War II, when Vega is employed in postal censorship, makes of all Americans one great majority in faith and determination. In his accounts of

Cuban revolutionaries and European socialists and Puerto Rican cigarmakers Bernardo Vega is telling us about the nation of immigrants of which they form a part.

Of the private concerns of Bernardo Vega we learn little. He tells us, impersonally, when he is out of work and when he finds work, when he is married, remarried, when he moves. But these details are simply dropped in passing. Vega assumes that what interests us is his role in the communal life and events that are his proper subject. The most personal, most lyrical passages in the *Memorias* are those revealing a man's love for New York: his first sight of the city from a pier on Staten Island; his first ride on a double-decker Fifth Avenue bus; the old open market, mostly Jewish then, on Park Avenue; free lunch counters in what used to be called saloons; Yorkville with its fine restaurants and lovely women; the luxurious speakeasies of prohibition days. No one who has ever lived there can fail to respond to the wonder and delight still fresh in these remembrances of the city. Some people have a notion that Hispanics are a foreign, disturbing presence in New York; Bernardo Vega shows that the city is theirs as much as anyone's, and perhaps more.

Vega's work was not published until 1977; despite its great documentary value, it does not seem to be widely known, as it deserves to be, outside Puerto Rico.[22]

Bernardo Vega and Jesus Colon must have known or at least known about each other in Puerto Rico or New York, but neither mentions the other in his book. This is surprising in the context of their ideological affinities. Colon's *A Puerto Rican in New York and Other Sketches*, a collection of personal essays, traces a life pattern remarkably similar to Vega's. Both men were born and grew up in the same mountain town, went to New York at roughly the same time, and dedicated their lives to helping the working classes through the furtherance of socialist ideals. Their introduction to those ideals came from the same sources; Colon describes how he used to listen through an open window to the reader in a cigar factory behind his home:

> I still hear this voice through the window of my childhood. Sometimes I listen to the same themes today, sometimes in Spanish, most of the time in English, from the

halls and squares of this New York of ours. Sometimes this voice comes through the radio, from Europe and Asia, crystallized now in pamphlets and books that have shaken the world to its foundations. But the theme is always the same, the same as the reader's from the cigarmaker's factory, coming to my home in my childhood's past.[23]

The "pamphlets and books that have shaken the world to its foundations" are the texts of Marxist communism, including Colon's own writings as columnist for the *Daily Worker*, where some of these sketches first appeared.

The most autobiographical of them are the early essays narrating Colon's emigration to New York as a sixteen-year-old stowaway during World War I and the hard years at unskilled labor that followed. Whereas Vega goes to New York at thirty years of age with a good trade and with social and political connections among his fellow Hispanics, Colon is thrown to sink or swim by himself on the heterogeneity of American life, an experience that explains a great deal about his later development: his dominance of English, for example, at least in writing, and his loyalty not simply to socialist ideas but to the institutionalization of those ideas in the Communist party. Colon is much more Americanized than Vega: he finds himself discriminated against as a black rather than as a Puerto Rican. When he shows up at an office to begin the translation job he had been offered by mail, the manager dismisses him with a quasi-apologetic "But I thought you were white."[24] A seemingly well-mannered little girl refuses the seat next to his at a luncheonette counter because "I won't sit beside no nigger."[25]

Abstractly, Colon's ideas about the social and political destiny of Puerto Rico are the same as Vega's: "Independence is the way that will provide for everything—material and spiritual—for the people of Puerto Rico. Independence and socialism. Socialism and independence."[26]

Like Vega, he is angered by the derogatory treatment of Puerto Ricans in the national press, which he proudly contrasts with the reliable information "published about the Puerto Ricans in our paper and in the progressive weekly and monthly publications."[27] He writes a series of semi-personal, semi-public tributes to individual Puerto Ricans, some well known ("The Story of Ana Roque," "My Personal Hall of Fame"), some personal friends ("Jose," "Marcelino"), and he denounces the bar slaying of veteran Bernardo Nunez "because he spoke Spanish" with his friends.[28] Despite the expressions of interest and concern, however, Colon's dedication to Puerto Rico and its people seems pale and impersonal beside Vega's. Colon shows very little interest in the Puerto Rican community in New York or in political and social developments on the Island. Nowhere does he mention taking part in demonstrations—as Vega did—on behalf of his compatriots. He warns against emigration in "Grandma, Please Don't Come!" but he obviously loves New York and would rather return to laissez-faire than to Cayey. He unquestionably believes what he writes, but he gives the impression of being motivated less by personal commitment than by a strong imperative to follow a party line in matters he would be expected to comment on.

Colon is much more doctrinaire than Vega and to that extent less interesting. He is too predictable. When he writes about capitalism, he describes it as "the system that is the source of all evil," as if he were developing or refining an insight into economic theory.[29] And when he describes how, at a workers' camp, "young and old—Jews, Italians, Negroes, Mexicans, Spaniards, Cubans, Chinese and Puerto Ricans . . . joined arms in twos, fours and sixes and started to sing and sing at the top of our voices to our heart's content,"[30] we seem to see ourselves looking at a remake based on an old, terribly dated scenario. Even the engaging "Carmencita," in which Colon's intolerant Catholic mother-in-law winds up praying that nothing will happen to Stalin, sacrifices what might have been a very good character study to a sterile bit of propaganda. But, although Colon includes in his book a number of essays squarely in the tradition of Addison and Steele, he does not ask to be judged in literary terms. His most important service is to reveal, through the example of his life, truths that one easily loses sight of in the messy collage of slums, violence, drugs, and welfare that satisfies the average New Yorker's curiosity about his Hispanic neighbors. He also serves to remind us that the intellectual forces that produced modern Cuba and modern Puerto Rico have roots that go deeper than Castro and Muñoz Marín.

In polar contrast to the books just described, Pedro Juan Labarthe's *The Son of Two Nations: The Private Life of a Columbia Student* is imbued with the faith and trust that have characterized in the national mythology the attitudes of those seeking a new life on our shores. Labarthe's opening paragraph could serve as the beginning of an ideal reconstruction of the immigrant experience:

> On the 12th of August of 1924 aboard of the S.S. "Porto Rico" which was headed for Brooklyn, Pedro Juan Labarthe saw for the first time the temptress of the greenhorn's eyes, Miss Liberty. He asked her blessing.[31]

Almost uniquely among the writings of Puerto Ricans who have settled on the mainland, Labarthe's book reflects the commitments of earlier immigrant literatures, to which it is indebted in spirit and design. Written in the third person in sometimes flawed English, it is the story of a poor boy, Pedro, who finds—as he came prepared to find—in the resources of the United States and in the generosity of its people fertile soil for his ambitions. The most interesting part of the book is the account of family background and schooling, which determined to a great extent the author's subsequent reactions during his college years in New York.

Pedro's father, son of an aristocratic Ponce family, had been indulged with the graces of European travel and broad humanistic education, advantages that he squanders on the genteel pursuit of women and the irresponsible enjoyment of declining fortunes. Widowed by his first wife, he marries Juanita, a pretty but illiterate young servant who accepts his proposal because he happens to be wealthier than her other suitor, a pharmacist. Soon after the birth of Pedro, their only child, the father drifts away from his mismatched wife into more congenial arms, leaving Juanita to bring the boy up as best she can on her meager income as a dressmaker. Despite this desertion, Pedro grows up in close touch with his father, and a mutually appreciative friendship develops between them during the son's adolescence.

Labarthe's parentage is significant in guiding the course of his political thinking during his formative years. Like most Island aristocrats, his father is anti-Yankee, a class attitude that has been studied with renewed interest in recent years.[32] The mother, belonging to a class that received recognition and hope under the new government, is strongly pro-American. The boy's discussions with both parents form the nucleus of a good basic analysis of Puerto Rican status, a more realistic and pragmatic analysis than would have been possible to anyone with strongly established convictions.

When Pedro graduates from the eighth grade in 1920, he is swept up by the resentments and revolutionary sentiments of his contemporaries: "There was a great political movement in those days. The youths were crying for independence. There was a deep hatred toward the Americans...who were looked upon as barbarians trying to murder the Island's culture, costumes, and psychology."[33] Some of the more immediate causes— and objects—of this hatred are the brawling sailors and insensitive Washington-appointed governors, who were like salt in the wounds of economic dependence and political domination.

Labarthe's youthful flirtation with independence is soon dampened by the quiet, rhetoric-free memories of his mother:

> She recalled the time when Porto Rico was under the Spanish domination. Schools were few and for the rich. Sanitation was poor. When an epidemic like cholera visited the Island it swept away thousands of lives. The Porto Rican did not have any freedom. They were under a Military Government. Freedom of the press was a myth.... Misery was everywhere and terror reigned on the Island.[34]

In his third year of high school Pedro meets some pro-American political leaders, including Juan B. Huyke, Emilio del Toro, and José Celso Barbosa. He becomes interested in their points of view and finds himself opposing his father's essentially emotional arguments for freedom:

> We are poor....I can not tell you whether we will have revolutions or not, but if there is no money in the Insular treasury and misery will be on the Island, revolutions are bound to come up then from bad to worse. We will run in line with some of our sister Latin Republics. We should

aspire to be something great in the world, and we alone cannot be. We should cling to that great nation that everyone is looking at as the richest in the world.[35]

Americans he comes to know personally also sway Pedro in their nation's favor: the women who come to his mother to have dresses made are courteous and fair in their payments; the owner of a provisions store in San Juan gives him a part-time job and enables him to continue his schooling; Mary White Bosworth, his high school English teacher, appears time and again in the book, bringing help and encouragement when needed. It is Miss Bosworth who advises Pedro, now in his last year of high school, to read *The Americanization of Edward Bok*, a real-life immigrant success story, which acts as a mold for the young man's aspirations. He writes to Bok and receives a generous reply, which reinforces the book's impression.

When he graduates from high school, Pedro is admitted to the University of Porto Rico. Because of his admiration for the United States, however, he petitions the local Department of Education for a scholarship to go north to study. Supported by Juan B. Huyke, the petition is granted. Pedro and his mother, whom he has renamed Ana, set sail for New York, where we left them in the opening paragraph.

The first news they receive in the new country is devastating: Pedro's scholarship has been canceled for lack of funds. Bitterly disappointed, with scant savings and inappropriate clothing, they determine to undergo whatever sacrifices are needed to achieve what they came for. Pedro soon gets a part-time job in a stockroom at Gimbel's, which he later supplements by working at the post office and tutoring in languages. Ana, who speaks no English, works as a seamstress but is continually running into problems, losing jobs, finding new ones, breaking down into the emotional equivalents of despair. Life must have been very hard at times for the young man and his mother, but Labarthe never allows the dark side of their experience to dominate his story. Hardships are not to be coddled but overcome; Pedro and Ana overcome them—through hard work, occasional hunger, persistence, and the good will of many people anxious to help a poor immigrant boy realize his concept of the American dream.

Labarthe is generous in recognizing all this help. While he was still in high school, Pedro had "lost all his suspicion on the sincerity of the Americans. They were sincere. They had a philanthropic mind. Those who wanted to be helped were helped by them."[36] He is delighted to keep discovering that "the bigger New York is the greater help you find in it."[37] For example, when Ana enters the Women's Hospital on 110th Street to be operated on for a cancerous ulcer, she and Pedro appeal to the hospital's Social Service Office for help, explaining that the $350 they have managed to save is for Pedro's education. The social worker is sympathetic; Ana doesn't pay a penny for her hospitalization. A little while later Dr. Hildreath, identified with Presbyterian Hospital in San Juan, treats Ana for a minor problem resulting from the operation. "Pedro...asked Dr. Hildreath for his bill. There was no bill. He was ready to help any Porto Rican when in need."[38]

Pedro often receives special consideration in his efforts towards a college degree. Mary White Bosworth, the high school English teacher, knows people at Columbia and is instrumental in getting him a scholarship there. When he fails trigonometry, he appeals to the dean, who makes arrangements for him to take geometry instead. He fails geometry and loses his scholarship but is rescued by a nice Swiss lady who gives him $75 to take—and pass—the course in the summer session. At a financially critical moment University Chaplain Knox gives him $50 to pay the rent. Once he is fired from the post office for what seems like a good reason; he pleads his case over the head of his immediate supervisor and is reinstated. When his supervisor at Gimbel's wants him to work hours that conflict with his classes, she receives orders to make special arrangements for him.

While we cannot fail to approve of the many acts of altruism he inspires, Pedro himself, in his unconditioned willingness to seek and accept favors wherever available, becomes progressively less attractive. The clear-eyed pragmatism of the poor boy in San Juan looks more like opportunism in the young Columbia student as the goal of success drifts slowly away from its mooring of hard work and self-reliance. Moreover, the desire to create a good impression to further his goals leads Pedro into little dishonesties of character, some of which he shares with the reader.

He "had to dress decently to be admitted to certain places where he could make advantageous friendships."[39] When he is required to list a religious preference on job applications, he is sorely perplexed:

> Sometimes he said "I am a Catholic" and would not be hired because the place was under Jewish or Protestant managements. Sometimes he said "I am a Protestant" and would not get the job because the place was under Catholic or Jewish managements and he decided to play his last card and said "I am a Spanish Jew" only to go away unemployed.[40]

More disturbing than these naively humorous disclosures are passages that suggest that Labarthe is being dishonest with the reader, if not with himself. When Pedro takes credit for making scholarships available to South American students, the lack of specific information is awkward. So is the absence of details to support his claim to have helped "hundreds of Porto Rican boys and girls" in the city:

> He had to write letters, recommend and go to the agencies, factories, institutions and corporations. The more they asked from him, the happier he felt. He inspired the Porto Rican youths, persuaded them to do their best, to be honest and work for the good of Porto Rico. He gave them advice and money.[41]

In the next paragraph Pedro tells us that he and Ana, on the verge of starvation, are unable to pay the rent—again.

The quotation above also illustrates Pedro's ingenuous, uncritical self-admiration and self-praise. The high school junior's exchange of letters with Edward Bok, based on an apparently honest conviction, is fine; but Pedro, having learned the trick, turns this type of exchange into a tedious form of name dropping. He tells of writing letters to Havelock Ellis, Blasco Ibañez, Concha Espina, Selma Lagerlöf, Fanny Hurst, the Crown Prince of Sweden, the brothers Alvarez Quintero, John Erskine, Cornelius Vanderbilt, Jr., and Michael Pupin, author of *From Immi-*

grant to Inventor. All of them write back, often enclosing their pictures; most become "good friends." At times the correspondences feature Pedro in more prominent roles. When he writes to Dr. Nicholas Murray Butler sympathizing with the latter's work on behalf of international peace, the great scholar "answered Pedro with a personal letter agreeing with him."[42] Pedro's once-mentioned articles for Spanish-American newspapers (exactly what they are about is not revealed) "brought forth congratulations from King Alfonso XIII."[43] At a time of particular strain between the United States and Latin America, Pedro writes a class paper proposing a Pan-American League of Nations to be set up in Porto Rico; he sends copies of the paper to Senator Borah, Eliju Root, William R. Shepard, Charles Cheney Hyde, Nicholas Murray Butler, and Edward Bok. Naturally,

> they all answered with personal letters agreeing with Pedro's point of view and helping him in the cause.
> Pedro saw the harvest of his work. Some of the marines were removed from Nicaragua. Mexican-American troubles were solved peacefully and the American public knew more about Porto Rico and the Latin Republics. Professor Shaw invited Pedro to read his article on Arbitration to the class on Latin American History and Pedro read it.[44]

There is, too, an unpleasing smugness in Pedro's assurance that "Prohibition is gaining ground and will survive"[45] and in his explanation of why he became a Republican and cast his maiden vote for Hoover over Smith.

For the most part Pedro's little offenses against humility and proportion are amusing, but they have the unfortunate result of making it hard to take Labarthe's book with the seriousness it deserves. *The Son of Two Nations* is one of the few works—the only one of its period—to speak for the undoubtedly large numbers of Puerto Rican migrants who embraced the traditional American dream and, like Labarthe, built successful, productive lives in the United States.[46] These people go largely unnoticed in the literature about Puerto Ricans on the mainland, an oversight questioned in a recent letter to the readers' page of the *San Juan Star*:

> Why is it that all studies, researches, observations, etc., about Puerto Ricans on the mainland are always on the negative side? Why hasn't there been a study of Puerto Ricans who left the island prior to the Depression in the United States for reasons of studying because it would facilitate their university education there and at the same time being able to work, or simply going to find a better life by struggling and working and not merely going to receive welfare funds.
>
> Why is it that no mention is ever made of how these Puerto Ricans of the 1920's, made it through hard work; incorporated themselves into the mainstream of life in the U.S., and, if you'll excuse the now "taboo term," assimilated an American life style, which I might add all immigrants in general have accomplished in the U.S.[47]

People who adapt successfully may be less interesting to write about than people who ostentatiously fail to adapt, but the writer of this letter is correct in attributing the scarcity of material on successful migrants partly to the strong resistence in Puerto Rico to cultural and linguistic assimilation to United States patterns. This resistence has become widespread in most social classes on the Island; it is particularly militant among the intellectuals, who set the patterns for describing the greatly increased migration following World War II.

NOTES

1. César Andreu Iglesias, ed., *Memorias de Bernardo Vega*, p. 106. Quotations in Spanish from this book and from those discussed in Chapter 2 are followed immediately by my translations in italics.
2. Ibid., p. 193.
3. Ibid., p. 250.
4. Ibid., p. 91.

5. Ibid., p. 120.
6. Ibid., p. 173.
7. Ibid., pp. 117, 165, 272.
8. Ibid., pp. 218-19.
9. In his introduction to the *Memorias* José Luis González traces this tension to opposed sources of independence sentiment in the Caribbean, one proletarian-revolutionary and the other romantic-reactionary. He continues to develop this theory in *El país de cuatro pisos y otros ensayos* (San Juan, Puerto Rico: Ediciones Huracán, 1980).
10. Vega, pp. 234-35.
11. Ibid., pp. 160, 245, 262-63.
12. Ibid., p. 156.
13. Ibid., pp. 49-50.
14. Ibid., p. 244.
15. Ibid., p. 131.
16. Ibid., p. 246.
17. Ibid., p. 143.
18. Ibid., pp. 198, 213.
19. "Hispanics are on the move around New York," *San Juan Star*, Portfolio Section, 23 November 1977, p. 1.
20. Vega, pp. 134, 136.
21. Ibid., p. 251.
22. *Monthly Review* has acquired the rights for the English version by Juan Flores, *The Memoirs of Bernardo Vega*.
23. Jesus Colon, *A Puerto Rican in New York*, p. 13.
24. Ibid., p. 51.
25. Ibid., p. 118.
26. Ibid., p. 202.
27. Ibid., pp. 9, 149, 157, 195.
28. Ibid., p. 126.
29. Ibid.
30. Ibid., p. 146.
31. Pedro Juan Labarthe, *The Son of Two Nations*, p. 15. Grammatical irregularities in Labarthe's English, his second language, will not be marked [*sic*].
32. See note 9 above.
33. Labarthe, p. 25.
34. Ibid., p. 26.
35. Ibid., p. 42.
36. Ibid., p. 46.
37. Ibid., p. 99.
38. Ibid., p. 90.

39. Ibid., p. 126.
40. Ibid., p. 135.
41. Ibid., p. 124.
42. Ibid., p. 161.
43. Ibid., p. 119.
44. Ibid., pp. 113-14.
45. Ibid., p. 165.
46. Richard Severo, "Faces of Change—Seeking Good Life in N.Y.," *San Juan Star*, 23 November 1977, p. 24.
47. Rosemarie Valentin, Letter, *San Juan Star*, 19 August 1981, p. 17.

2

VIEWS FROM AN ISLAND

The parents of Eduardo, in Pedro Juan Soto's *Ardiente suelo, fría estación*, belonged to the poor, unskilled, inarticulate generation that migrated to New York in unprecedented numbers during the decade following World War II, drawn by job opportunities, low air fares, and the expectation of help from those who had already pioneered the way. Unable to speak English, most of them lodged behind ghetto walls of hostility and fear. Older residents saw them as a blight, social technicians as a problem. Eduardo recalls the want of humanity in the way in which even his best-intentioned teachers defined him for themselves:

> Cuando más, una cifra de estadística, un producto de una región subdesarrollada, tal vez una reliquia a la cual había que escudar del manoseo profano y de las mentes no entendidas en antropología. Ellos, pues, eran sus descubridores, sus tutores, sus historiadores, ya que aquellas *cosas* no podían definirse por sí mismas, cuidarse a sí mismas, expresar su propia historia.
>
> *At most, a statistical digit, product of an underdeveloped area, perhaps a fossil to be guarded from profane handling and from minds not versed in anthropology. For they were his discoverers, his tutors, his historians, since those objects could not define themselves, take care of themselves, write their own history.*[1]

What Edurado has no way of knowing is that his people's history was being recorded at the time by sympathetic, understanding observers—insular Puerto Rican writers who visited and lived in the metropolis and sought to capture in stories, plays, and novels the lifestyles of their Island's greatest colony.

These writers are not completely objective chroniclers, nor do they see in the migration the same meanings and patterns that the migrants themselves perceive. They are middle-class intellectuals writing about the unschooled and socially marginal; they are writing for an audience that has had little contact with the migrants at home or abroad; they often view the migration within a framework of moral and cultural values that would have been but dimly recognized by hundreds and thousands of migrants washing dishes and running elevators for money to buy plastic-covered furniture on the installment plan and keep their children in public school. On the other hand, this moral and cultural frame adds to their work a philosophic glow, which illuminates areas of human experience inaccessible to the probes of naturalism. The first four books discussed below evidence the idealism so prominent in this literature, while the last four illustrate differences in attitudes toward the material or in the ways in which it is used.

Enrique Laguerre's powerful symbol of a tropical ceiba tree planted—with its massive truck and great buttress roots—in a flowerpot has a broad range of significance in his novel *La ceiba en el tiesto*. It is variously interpreted by Doña María to suggest memories of rural Puerto Rico, the pressures that forced her and her family to leave the Island, the impossibility of transplanting a way of life, and a fear that something has been lost and will never be replaced:

> —Verá usted—deciame. —En la Isla somos una gran familia pobre, apretujada en una casita, pero se vive. . . . En la finca de casa había una ceiba. Por las tardes y en los días de fiesta, a veces, nos reuníamos alli los amigos y los parientes. . . . Cuando ya no me quendó mas escapatoria que vender la finca para venir a esta ciudad, me dijé: "Voy a llevar la ceiba en un tiesto." Como que me rompo con solo pensar en el imposible.
> —*You see—she used to say to me—on the Island we're one big family, poor and cramped into a little shack, but we live. . . . On*

*our farm there was a ceiba tree. In the evening and on holidays
sometimes we'd get together there, friends and relatives.... Finally
when there was no other way out for me but to sell the farm to
come to this city, I said to myself: "I'll take the ceiba along in a
flowerpot." I sort of get all broken up just thinking of how impossible it was.*[2]

What forced Doña María and so many others to leave their beloved home was Puerto Rico's overpopulation, growing like ceiba
roots in the flowerpot of the Island's resources: "Me apena que
tengamos que vivir tan lejos del país. Ya no cabemos en el" [*I'm
sorry we have to live so far from our country. We don't fit there
any more*].[3]

Doña María's regret at having had to leave Puerto Rico for New
York is not merely a form of nostalgia or a reaction against cold
weather, slums, and prejudice. For Laguerre, New York not
only worsens the quality of the migrants' lives, it threatens their
moral integrity as well. Gustavo, the protagonist of the novel,
commenting on a group of drunken Puerto Ricans singing off-
color songs on the beach at Coney Island, says, "La verdad es
que nos hemos perdido aquí" [*The truth is we've lost our bearings
here*].[4] One implication of his remark is that Puerto Ricans who
migrate run the danger of losing an old ethic without acquiring a
new one. But there is also the suggestion, reinforced elsewhere,
that the new cultural environment contains elements that are
morally corrosive in a more absolute sense. There is a particularly revealing passage later in the novel: Gustavo, having gradually degenerated into a bum (for other reasons than simply
being in New York), is living from handouts on the Bowery.
One day he sees a fellow Puerto Rican and asks him for the
"loan" of a dollar. The other replies, "No creí a un paisano capaz
de estar en el Bowery. Retírese de ahí. Eso es cosa de americanos.
La pobreza nuestra es de otro tipo." [*I didn't believe anyone from
back home could wind up on the Bowery. Get away from here. This is for
Americans; our poverty is a different kind*].[5] "Our" poverty is presumably the decent, bucolic poverty described by Doña María,
poverty softened by the love of family and friends and by the
support of healthy moral traditions. "American" poverty is urban—

characterized by squalor, loneliness, and the absence of human warmth. Like many writers in Puerto Rico, a recently industrialized community, Laguerre uses the romantic city/country dichotomy to structure his moral vision. In this connection, Wordsworth's description of London's Bartholomew Fair in Book VII of *The Prelude* is remarkably analogous to Gustavo's reactions to Coney Island:

> Todo me estuvo destartalado, brutal y sucio. Era un compendio de todo lo morboso y malsano que perturba al hombre: exhibiciones de seres anormales, máquinas que ponían en ridículo al prójimo, juegos violentos, un museo de cera horripilante, y suciedad, papeles y tragaderos de monedas; voces y ruidos desagradables....
> La multitud iba y venia comiendo, gritando, riendose desaforadamente. Nunca había visto tanta fealdad atropellada en tan pequeño espacio.
> *It all seemed to me disordered, brutal, and dirty. It was an abstract of everything sick and morbid that troubles mankind: freak shows, machines to make people look ridiculous, violent rides, a horrifying wax museum, and dirt, papers, and slot machines; shouting and harsh noises....*
> *The mob came and went, eating, yelling, laughing impulsively. I had never seen so much ugliness trampled into such a little space.*[6]

Also in keeping with the romantic judgment of the city is Laguerre's emphasis on the mechanistic quality of life in New York, "la ciudad de los incontables ídolos mecánicos" [*the city of innumerable mechanical idols*][7] where "la realidad mecánica nos abruma" [*the mechanical reality crushes us*].[8]

An even stronger statement on New York as the dead end of mechanistic civilization is René Marqués's drama *La carreta*, the classic expression in Puerto Rican literature of the theme of country-to-city migration. The first act introduces a poor country family preparing to leave their unproductive farm and move to San Juan, where Luis, the breadwinner, hopes to work in a factory. Central to the first act is the ideological conflict between the grandfather, who has an almost mystical attachment to the land

and an unshakable belief in its redemptive powers, and Luis, who has a similar faith in machines. Act II records the deterioration of the family in La Perla, a San Juan slum. With the grandfather's death the mother, Doña Gabriela, has become the family's moral focus; it is she who absorbs the pain of her younger son's arrest for stealing and her daughter's attempted suicide after a kitchen abortion. Luis, after a series of factory layoffs, has turned to gardening, to the land, to support the family.

Act III takes place a year later in New York, the Mecca of Juan's machine-inspired visions. The accelerated decline of the family is physically apparent. Juan, though he boasts somewhat defiantly about his job in a boiler factory, is nervous and unresponsive. Doña Gabriela seems to be turning old before her children's eyes: "aquí se noh ehtá doblando como una caña sin agua. Se noh ehtá arrugando como un pajuilito seco.... El pelo se le ehtá poniendo del mehmo color de ehte cielo americano" [*here she's bendin' over on us like a dry weed. She's wrinklin' up like a dry cashew husk.... Her hair's turnin' the same color as this American sky*].[9] Throughout this act New York is spoken of as cold, mechanized, lonely, empty of pity and love—like the machines to which Luis turns ever more desperately in his quest for a faith that will replace the grandfather's. Finally, in a burlesque martyrdom, Luis is caught in the machinery of the boiler factory and killed. Doña Gabriela determines to ship the body back to Puerto Rico for burial and to return to work the land:

> Porque ahora me doy cuenta lo que noh pasaba a toh. ¡La mardisión de la tierra! La tierra es sagrá. La tierra no se abandona....Y yo vuervo con miijo a la tierra de onde salimoh. Y hundiré mis manoh en la tierra colorá de mi barrio....Y mis manoh volverán a ser fuerteh....Eh tierra que da vía.
> *Because now I understand what was happenin' to all of us. The curse of the land! The land is sacred. You don't desert the land....And I'm goin' back with my little boy to the land we left behind. And I'll sink my hands into the red earth were I come from....And my hands will be strong again....The land gives life.*[10]

A return to Puerto Rico, not necessarily to the land this time, is a prominent goal in J. L. Vivas Maldonado's *A vellón las esperanzas, o Melania*, a collection of stories interrelated by common characters and setting and by frequent references to Melania, a fascinating whore who makes good by marrying a rich Jew and moving from the South Bronx to an apartment downtown. Like Laguerre and Marqués, Vivas Maldonado feels that Puerto Ricans change somehow when they migrate to New York: "Que si los puertorriqueños cambian aquí es cosa vieja" [*That Puerto Ricans change here's an old story*].[11] For the most part they change for the worse, and their deterioration is progressive. The male prostitutes will respond ever less vibrantly to the excitement of Broadway night after night. The cuckholded college graduate who drinks to near insensibility will eventually manage, through courage or accident, to kill himself. The macho who takes his woman back will drop her again, lower next time. And the tired, suffering neighbors will continue to ask Hermana Suncha to ask the spirits what went wrong.

In contrast to all this human waste is the blind singer Antero, an independentist and the only idealized figure in the book. Antero first apears in "Jilguero de calle abajo," a dramatic script with authorial asides, where he maintains a sense of integrity that his compatriots have completely lost sight of in the moral miasma that engulfs them. He refuses to apply for relief, for example, an attitude incomprehensible to two of the spiritually blind:

HOMBRE (núm. 1):
Mas lo que coge del rilih, ¿no?
ANTERO:
No, no estoy en relief.
HOMBRE (núm. 2):
¡Ay, deja esa guasimilla! ¿Que tú no te aprovechas pa sacarle dinero a ehtos condenaos?
ANTERO:
No, trabajo pa vivir. Ayudo al super a dar estín, mapeo el jol. . .lo que sea. . .
Los do hombres
quedan en silencio.
Una gran duda se
refleja en sus rostros.

HOMBRE (núm. 1):
Toh los días se tira uno a la calle. ¡Mira y que ciego y no está en rilih! ¡Ay, bendito! Si fuera yo, me tendrían que dar hasta la comida. Mira, mi viejo, si eso es ahí, en la 125. Vete por allí, y pide, que pa eso éste es el país más rico del mundo. Y mas tú, que estás que buhcas y no te encuentrah.

ANTERO:
Yo soy de Puerto Rico....

Man #1
Besides what you get from relief, eh?

ANTERO
No, I'm not on relief.

Man #2
Ah, don't pull my leg! You don't cash in on the money you can get from these bastards?

ANTERO:
No, I work for a living. I help the super with the furnace, mop the hall...anything...

The two men
remain silent.
Their faces reflect
a serious doubt.

Man #1
Every day you find one on the street. Look at that—blind and not on relief! If it was me, they'd even have to feed me. Look, buddy, it's right over there on 125 Street. Go on over there and ask. That's why this is the richest country in the world. And especially you, who can't even find yourself when you're looking'.

ANTERO:
I'm from Puerto Rico....[12]

If Antero's refusal to accept government handouts sounds unreal, it might be noted that the Puerto Rico Independence party, even while struggling for enough votes to remain officially registered, opposed the application of the federal food stamp program to Puerto Rico.[13] It is Antero who, at the close of the book, boards a plane for San Juan after a heated argument with a statehooder who sees the United States as one huge relief agency: "A mí que me den comida, dinero, ropa y seguridad económica. Y ustedes pueden quedarse con todo ese paquete de ideales y de libertad y de república" [*Let them give me food, clothes and financial security. And you can keep that whole pack of ideals about freedom and the republic*].[14]

Melania is a good example of how among Puerto Rican writers language is used as a barometer of moral and cultural solvency in *la colonia*. In the conversation between Antero and the two men on the merits of relief, for example, Antero's standard diction contrasts with the others' aspiration or loss of final *s*, a usage considered substandard. They address Antero with the informal second personal pronoun, while he addresses them, individually, with the formal third personal pronoun, the polite use under the circumstances. Antero even speaks better English than they do, if one judges by his *relief* compared to their *rilih*! Elsewhere, in authorial asides, Vivas Maldonado describes the Spanish heard in the South Bronx as "distinto y quebrado" [*different, broken*][15] and invites the reader to share his disapproval of anglicisms like *yarda* and *rufo*: "¡Que Español! Terrible, ¿no?" [*What Spanish! Awful, isn's it?*].[16]

Another book concerned with cultural shift is Guillermo Cotto-Thorner's *Trópico en Manhattan*, which explores "el ambiente cosmopólito de la ciudad en la cual el puertorriqueño se siente baja la amenaza constante de perder su idioma y sus tradiciones" [*the cosmopolitan atmosphere of the city, in which the Puerto Rican feels he's in constant danger of losing his language and his traditions*].[17] The hero of the book is Juan Marcos Villalobos, a young sociology teacher who has come to New York to do graduate work and return to the Island better prepared to help his people. While working in the Forty-Second Street library Juan founds the Eugenio María de Hostos Club to help preserve Puerto Rico's culture and language in New York and to make that culture known to the general public. The thesis aspect of the novel is balanced by a melodramatic plot centered on the rivalry between Antonio and Lencho, a rivalry that began in Puerto Rico and has little to do with New York. Much more interesting than the plot are the author's comments, made both directly and through his characters, on the cultural and moral climate through which these characters move.

Cotto-Thorner's observations parallel those of Laguerre, Marqués, and Vivas-Maldonado. The statement "Nueva York atomiza" [*New York atomizes*][18] suggests the disintegration of what is essentially human. When Eudosia goes insane, she is linked to the "miles de compatriotas que tambien habían sufrido la atrofia de la razón en el herbidero indecifrable de la metrópolis" [*thousands of compatriots who have also suffered mental atrophy in the incomprehensible swarm of the metropolis*].[19] The power of the city to deaden mind and spirit is embodied in a vivid presentation of its noises:

Tranvías, autobuses, automóviles, carros de caballos, camiones, trenes, bicicletas, motorcicletas, aviones, carretillas, bombas de incendio con sus potentes motores y sus alarmantes sirenas, gritería de muchachos y mayores, zumbido de conversación en el hormiguero de las aceras, risotadas, imprecaciones, pregones, el estallido de un motor que falla, ruedas sobre rieles que trituran el sociego, berbiquí de hélices talandro atronadamente el espacio; ruido, ruido, RUIDO: Nueva York.

Trolleys, buses, cars, horse-drawn wagons, trucks, trains, bicycles, motorcycles, planes, wheelbarrows, fire trucks with their powerful motors and frightening sirens, shouts of children and adults, buzz of conversation in the anthill of streets, outbursts of laughter, curses, loudspeakers, the backfiring of a motor, wheels on rails grinding tranquility, propellers drilling thunderously through space; noises, noise, NOISE: New York.[20]

Language—preoccupation with the retention of good Spanish— is another major theme here. On his first date with Miriam, a Puerto Rican girl who has lived in New York for twenty of her twenty-two years, Juan is most struck by the fact that she speaks "un español tan correcto" [*such good Spanish*],[21] and Eurípidez Pérez is criticized because his daughters hardly speak the mother tongue.[22] Amusingly, the villains of the piece all speak a Spanish corrupted by the frequent use of English word borrowings. Lencho cannot hold a job because of his inability to speak English, but in ten lines of dialogue on page forty-seven he uses the terms *yobsito, bosa, chequeandome, raque*, and *bigchot*, all borrowed from English and adapted to Spanish morphology. Like Vivas Maldonado, Cotto-Thorner provides his readers with a glossary of what he calls *Neoyorkismos*—a lovely coinage!

Cotto-Thorner goes further than most other writers in describing the emotional attachment his characters feel for the mother country-fatherland. When Juan arrives in New York, at the home of Antonio and Finí, the excitement of seeing the city and visiting the mainland for the first time is completely overshadowed by the nostalgia he feels for the country he left some hours before. Finí's cooking makes of their apartment a little piece of the beloved homeland:

> Olía a Puerto Rico. El arroz con pollo, las habichuelas coloradas, la ensalada de aguacate, las aceitunas regorditas, los tostones, el dulce de guyaba con quesito blanco, y el café prieto, unían sus perfumes en una sinfonía nostálgica de la patria ausente.... Aquella hospitalidad, aquella dulzura, aquella comunión invisible que lo unía a los que ahora con el compartían el pan, lo emocionó tanto, que sintió que lagrimas nublaban sus ojos.
>
> *It smelled of Puerto Rico. The chicken and rice, the red beans, the avocado salad, the plump olives, the plantain fritters, the guava jam with white cheese, and the black coffee joined their perfumes in a nostalgic symphony of the absent fatherland.... That hospitality, that sweetness, that invisible communion which united him to those who were now sharing their bread with him moved him so much that he felt his eyes cloud with tears.*[23]

Juan weeps again later in the novel when, walking through his first snowfall, he hears a Puerto Rican Christmas carol playing from a juke box in a Puerto Rican eatery.

The persistence of close emotional ties with homeland language and culture is one of the reasons for the relative self-containment of New York's Puerto Rican minority and has undoubtedly muted the urge toward Americanization, which was so conspicuous among earlier groups of migrants. Self-containment has also been encouraged by the size of the Hispanic community, the easy communication between the Island and its *colonia*, and the city's efforts to accommodate the new arrivals through special education programs, bilingual personnel, and so forth. Of the four books discussed above, only Laguerre's—because its plot requires that the protagonist avoid Hispanic neighborhoods—shows much interaction between Puerto Ricans and *americanos*. Elsewhere non-Puerto Ricans—cops, landlords, bosses, and the like—are present only by reference. For Cotto-Thorner, at least, self-containment is all to the good, the sociological concomitant of cultural survival:

> En esa parte del Parque Central nadie habla inglés; todo es "puro boricua". Es la sustitución adecuada de la plaza de armas de los ausentes pueblitos de la isla.
> *In that section of Central Park nobody speaks English; everything is pure Puerto Rican. It's a satisfying substitute for the plazas left behind in the little Island towns.*[24]

Sentiments like these are probably felt to some degree by most people who leave their homes for alien places. On the other hand, it should be kept in mind that the authors quoted here were not really immigrants: they were insular Puerto Ricans writing for an insular Puerto Rican audience at a period when the charismatic Luis Muñoz Marín was fomenting cultural nationalism as a fortifying element in the Island's magnificent effort to rescue itself from centuries of poverty, aimlessness, and exploitation. Small wonder that many Puerto Ricans hoped their migrating countrymen would resist the forces of assimilation that were being so successfully trounced on the Island's intellectual beachheads.

Fortunately, not all books written by Puerto Rican authors about New York are idealistic or judgmental. Pedro Juan Soto's *Spiks*, regarded as one of the best short-story collections published in Puerto Rico, is about immigrants whose Spanish is too poor to be considered corruptible and whose culture no one could wish to preserve. Thwarted by physical, educational, and psychological limitations, Soto's characters are stripped to human basics; they happen to be Puerto Ricans in New York, but they could have been Poles, blacks, or Italians living in Marseilles, Liverpool, or Berlin. The opening story of *Spiks* takes place in a San Juan airport, where a seventeen-year-old girl is being sent to a brother in New York to keep her from continuing an affair with her sister's weak-spirited husband. Life for her up north will be simply an extension of the life she is leaving, with little more than physical distance between them. There is only one story in this book where a moral distinction is drawn between the two environments. "Los inocentes" is about a young woman who is determined to have her brother, an adult idiot, committed to a public asylum despite the pleas and arguments of their mother, who retains traces of an ethic that is bound geographically:

> —En Puerto Rico no hubiera pasao ehto.—Eh Puerto Rico era dihtinto—dijo Hortensia, hablando por encima del hombro—. Lo conocía la gente. Podía salir porque lo conocía la gente. Pero en Niu Yol la gente no se ocupa y uno no conoce al vecino. La vida eh dura. Yo me paso los añoh cose que cose y todavía sin casalme.
> —*In Puerto Rico this wouldn't have happened.—In Puerto Rico it was different—said Hortensia, speaking over her shoulder—. People knew him, He could go out because people knew him. But in New York people don't care and don't know their neighbors. Life is tough. I've been sewing away year after year and I'm still not married.*[25]

A distinction is made, but in the context of the brother-son's growing violence and recent attempt on the mother's life, no simple judgment is suggested.

If migration does not play a determining role in the lives of Soto's characters, why does he bring them to New York? With very little modification the same stories could have been set in towns and cities on the island. Why didn't he leave them there? Without pretending to reproduce the author's exact intentions, one can see a twofold usefulness in the New York setting for this book. First, realistic portrayal of the types of people Soto writes about is practically unknown in earlier Puerto Rican literature; they were not the stuff literature was expected to be made of. But Island readers were familiar with similar character types in realistic urban literature from Europe and the United States; it was therefore easier for them to accept Soto's people in an environment associated with a realistic literary tradition. Second, Soto's characters are the socially marginal people who remain curiously invisible to members of other classes within their own society: we all learn to edit out parts of our surroundings, including other people. By placing these edited-out people against an unfamiliar background, Soto forces his readers to see them. He makes the familiar visible.

The same kind of perception editing accounts in part for the impressions of New York in the books discussed earlier. Cotto-Thorner is appalled at the noise of New York; New Yorkers are usually appalled at the noise pollution they find in San Juan. Vivas Maldonado is shocked at the tenements "olorosos a cucarachas" [*smelling of rats and roaches*][26] where the immigrants are forced to live; he seems unaware of the slums they left behind. In these authors and in Laguerre and Marqués perceptions are edited into moral statements. Soto, on the other hand, forces his readers to see what was edited out as a guide to self-perception.

The polar opposite of *Spiks* in subject matter and technique is Amelia Agostini de del Río's *Puertorriqueños en Nueva York*, which is about a small, relatively comfortable minority. Born into a well-to-do family in a small town in southwestern Puerto Rico, del Río studied at Vassar, Columbia, and Madrid and spent most of her professional life teaching and directing the Spanish Department at Barnard. Her New York is obviously not El Barrio; her characters would feel uneasily out of place there. The opening story of this delightful collection is narrated by an antique marbletop table which, when its owner dies in Yauco, is sent to the owner's already elderly daughter in New York, assured there of a continued place in the family's care and affection. Most of del Río's characters are like that little table. They live as most of them must have lived in their small towns on the Island, gossiping, laughing, remembering, warm in sympathy and rich in traditions that remain vigorous in their new soil. Most of these people relate well to the city, settling inconspicuously into its ways; some may feel a bit of notalgia for Puerto Rico now and then, but they seldon speak of returning. Only in one story, "Añorar...y callar...," about a racially mixed marriage, does del Río deal with the problems of poverty and prejudice that loom so large in most of the literature on Puerto Ricans in New York.

Del Río deserves wider recognition than she has received for her short stories. Her preferred point of view is that of the omniscient author with full rights of commentary over her characters. This is not a convention likely to enflame contemporary criticism, but it is right for her. It allows her to create a brilliant interplay of humor and sympathy through exceptional linguistic resources rooted in the idioms of her native land and polished by a lifetime of intimacy with Spanish literature. She writes mostly about common, undramatic events, but is forceful in her infrequent expressions of great passion. "Aquel Potro Salvaje" makes a beautiful comment on love in two and a half pages and ends with a powerful statement on life and death:

> Olvidaré que ha muerto viejecillo, inconsciente, casi transformado en vegetal, ¡aquel hombre que era un potro salvaje, fogoso, libre, a galope siempre por la serranía y por la sabana y por la vida!
>
> *I will forget that he died a little old man, unconscious, turned almost vegetable—that man who was a wild colt, spirited and free, forever galloping over mountain and over plain and over life!*[27]

The most comprehensive treatment of the Puerto Rican migration to New York is Manuel Méndez Ballester's *Encrucijada*, first presented at the 1959 Puerto Rican Theater Festival. Embracing three generations, the play touches in an organized way upon the prototypical experiences of the migrants, the ideological backdrop to their attitudes toward the United States, and the changes they undergo in the new land. Méndez Ballester sees the Barrio period as temporary and transitory in the classic process of adaptation to a new way of life. This transitoriness is dramatized in the opposition between Mario, a Nationalist involved in terrrorist activities, and his older brother Felipe, who boasts of being "con los americanos ciento por ciento" [*with the Americans a hundred percent*][28] and who is responsible for having brought Mario and their parents and sister to New York. Felipe insists that the family learn to assimilate; Mario wants them to return to Puerto Rico. Both are aware that change will occur in one direction or the other.

Neither Mario nor Felipe can be considered the hero of *Encrucijada*. Neither is particularly attractive as a persona, and both are to some extent confused and inconsistent. Mario at one time criticizes Felipe's Spanish and at another time tells him, "¡Lastima que hables tan mal el inglés!" [*Too bad you speak such lousey English!*].[29] Despite his anti-Americanism Mario is in love with an American girl, Lorna, who is pregnant by him. The political discussions between Felipe and Mario and their father illustrate, in their contrasting approaches to United States-Puerto Rican relations, Méndez Ballester's two most noteworthy achievements in this play: his dispassionate presentation of opposing ideas and his exploration of the frequently self-interested motivations behind idelogical commitments. A sense of balance and detachment functions as a counterpoint to the dramatic movement. While the family complain about anti-Puerto Rican prejudice in housing, their neighbor Chana shouts obscenities, throws garbage out the window, and drowns out their conversation with her blaring radio. The 100 percent American Felipe loses his job at a garage when he tries to stop his 100 percent American boss from beating up a defenseless black. Jack, the American janitor, does his best to keep life tolerable for the Puerto Rican tenants in the decaying tenement owned by a Puerto Rican who lives in Miami. It is difficult to pass judgment in Méndez Ballester's Barrio.

And it is difficult to pass judgment on the play's epilogue, which takes place seven years after Mario's arrest at the close of the third act. Alfonso is trying to persuade his grandson, Mario's and Lorna's child, to speak Spanish to him, which the youngster manages with some difficulty and great reluctance. Mario is to be released the following month, and he and Lorna plan to resettle in Miami with their son. Felipe has married and moved to the Bronx. Marta, the sister, is living in Chicago with her husband Antonio, once a boarder with the family. Jack and Chana have gotten together and are preparing to leave for Texas with Luis, Chana's trouble-prone son from a previous marriage. The author seems to be sending them all off with his blessing, hoping that Mario will learn to control his temper, Felipe his gambling, Chana her vulgarity. Puerto Rico is seven years farther away; the migrants are moving on.

The most recent book written by a Puerto Rican about the New York migration takes the materials that have become standard fare in such literature—the dehumanized city, violence, slums, prejudice, and on and on—and shapes them in new and highly interesting ways. Emilio Díaz Valcárcel's *Harlem todos los días* is a comic satire about the city as seen through the eyes of Gerardo, a somewhat naive young man recently arrived from the Island. Gerardo is the traditional visitor-from-abroad whose clear eyes can still form fresh perspectives on the world around him; he is also the young man from the country learning about life in the metropolis. His mentor is the fabulous Aleluya, also from Puerto Rico but so completely sui generis that he repudiates all patterns. The New York presented in this novel is not limited by class or neighborhood: it is a microcosm peopled from a vast palette of social, national, and racical backgrounds. The Puerto Ricans here have a positive, aggressive image of themselves as citizens of a city they have made their own. As Bigote tells Gerardo,

—Si no te gusta el Barrio, te puedes mudar al Bronx o al Bajo Manhattan. Ya Long Island está cayendo y empezamos a invadir Queens. Estamos llenando casi todo el West Side. Un día nos vamos a quedar con la ciudad.
—*If you don't like El Barrio, you can move to the Bronx or Lower Manhattan. Long Island's already falling, and we're starting to invade Queens. We're filling up practically the whole West Side. Some day the city'll be ours.*[30]

This is a new note in the literature about El Barrio, a door opening out from the claustrophobic ghetto into a world of vitality and confidence. Díaz Valcárcel's characters may live in El Barrio, but they spread out and move easily among blacks, Spaniards, Chinese, Poles, Greeks, Africans, Koreans—even well-heeled gringos. By following them through their multifaceted activities and contacts the author constructs a wonderfully exhilarating impression of today's New York and, increasingly, today's America. It is a largely comic and satiric impression, to be sure, but these modes hold their own truth.

Published in 1978, *Harlem todos los días* sees New York very differently from the other books described in this chapter, most of which were published nearly a quarter century earlier. Its focus is also different in that it treats the city's Puerto Ricans as literary raw material rather than as a cause for moral or cultural concern. It is like the earlier books in that it views New York through the eyes of Spanish-speaking immigrants created by a writer born and raised in Puerto Rico. The following chapters will describe the quite different perceptions of Puerto Ricans made in America.

NOTES

1. Pedro Juan Soto, *Ardiente suelo, fría estación*, p. 121
2. Enrique Laguerre, *La ceiba en el tiesto*, pp. 51-52.
3. Ibid., p. 49.
4. Ibid., p. 52.
5. Ibid., p. 64.
6. Ibid., p. 50.
7. Ibid., p. 65.
8. Ibid., p. 49.
9. René Marqués, *La carreta*, p. 487.
10. Ibid., pp. 561-62.
11. J. L. Vivas Maldonado, *A vellón las esperanzas, o Melania*, p. 66.
12. Ibid., p. 57.
13. Antero is clearly a minority figure and the PIP (Partido Independentista Puertorriqueño) a minority party: more than half the families in Puerto Rico receive food stamps.
14. Vivas Maldonado, p. 106.
15. Ibid., p. 77.
16. Ibid., p. 80.
17. Guillermo Cotto-Thorner, *Trópico en Manhattan*, p. 42.
18. Ibid., p. 25.
19. Ibid., p. 142.
20. Ibid., p. 19.
21. Ibid., p. 65.
22. Ibid., p. 71.
23. Ibid., p. 22.
24. Ibid., p. 143.
25. Pedro Juan Soto, *Spiks*, p. 41.
26. Vivas Maldonado, p. 5.
27. Amelia Agostini de del Río, *Puertorriqueños en Nueva York*, p. 89.
28. Manuel Méndez Ballester, *Encrucijada*, p. 84.
29. Ibid., p. 52.
30. Emilio Díaz Valcárcel, *Harlem todos los días*, p. 17.

3

PIRI THOMAS

Piri Thomas was born in Harlem Hospital in 1928, the first important Puerto Rican writer with no umbilical cord to the Island and the first using English as a native language to describe the labor of constructing a personal interpretation of American life from the concrete and asphalt of El Barrio. His three important books—*Down These Mean Streets*, *Seven Long Times*, and *Savior, Savior, Hold My Hand*—make up an overlapping narrative of his life in Spanish Harlem and in various prisons from the late 1930s to the early 1960s. Despite stylistic and structural weaknesses in his writing and a general narrowness in the range of experience described, Thomas remains, because of the persistent moral commentary which runs through his work, the most serious and interesting spokesman for second-generation Puerto Ricans in New York, even for those who deplore the image he projects and the willingness of readers and reviewers to accept his autobiographical narratives as accurate generalized descriptions of what it's like to grow up Nuyorican.

The books are autobiographical, but it is important to distinguish in them between author and persona. Although Thomas does not always achieve the necessary disengagement from his past to handle his earlier life with complete objectivity—*Down These Mean Streets*, in particular, is flawed with inappropriate editorializing—he tries not to mitigate his failings, so the younger Piri Thomas is often a very unattractive figure, even to his re-creator. The relationship between author and subject is curious and deserves careful attention of the reader. What Thomas does, in fact, is to use the data of his life as a text on which to base an increasingly impersonal parable on the poor and the marginal in the United States. In order to keep the author-persona relationship clear in this chapter, the author will be called Thomas, the persona Piri.

Down These Mean Streets, though it is the most self-involved of Thomas's books, describes in detail many of the experiences which have come to be regarded as typical of the Nuyorican way of life. Piri grows up during the depression and war years, conscious of "Poppa's" hard struggle to support a wife and five children and vaguely intrigued by "Momma's" nostalgic memories of the Puerto Rico she and Poppa had left in search of a better life. Piri's visits to the welfare office as Momma's interpreter, his discipline problems at school, the hero worship of Jack Armstrong and Scarface, the beatings (one almost ending in blindness) from the kids on the Italian block, the need to be "hombre" and show "heart," gang wars, drugs, sex challenges, petty crime—these are the sort of data Thomas draws on to sketch Piri's early formation.

Underlying and uniting the data is the theme that runs through all of Thomas: the painful job of recognizing and then accepting oneself in a world of confusing norms and tangled ideologies. Where can the immigrant's son turn for guidance through this brand new, uncompromising landscape? Momma's green Puerto Rico is invisible in the grey Harlem streets, and Poppa, grateful for the insecure tenantry of whatever niche the alien world allows him, has neither the experience nor the spiritual resources to guide his first-born.

Outside the home there is school, traditional guide on the passage to the American way of life. But Piri's way of life is not the traditional American way: it is El Barrio, poverty and prejudice, the crippling burden of being both "spic" and "nigger" at a time when few people had heard of ethnic consciousness or the rights of minorities. School has led many from that sort of darkness to a place in the sun. For Piri it doesn't work.

A third blueprint is the paraworld of the street, where young dropouts from the larger world form their own societies out of rigorous, clearly defined codes that provide a needed sense of identity and belonging. Gang membership is extremely demanding; each gang is a little fascist state, ethnically organized, violence oriented, loveless, paranoid, sadistic. Membership, won by proving heart through an act of physical or moral outrage, is maintained at the sometimes enormous cost of meeting continual challenges, mostly arbitrary and malicious, from within the group. Piri's sordid visit to a homosexual pad is brought on by one such challenge:

> There were some improbable stories of exploits with faggots. Then one stud, Alfred, said, "Say, man, let's make it up to the faggots' pad and cop some bread."
>
> We all looked at him. He was a little older—not much, but enough to have lived the extra days it takes to learn the needed angles.
>
> "Whadda you cats think?" he said. "Oh, shit, don't tell me you ain't down."
>
> Eyes shifted, feet scratched gravel, fingers poked big holes in noses—all waiting to see who would be the first to say, "Yeah, man, let's make it."
>
> The stud snapped his fingers, as if to say, "Motherfuckers, who's a punk?" Nobody, man. Without a word we jumped off the stoop and, grinning, shuffled toward the faggots' building.[1]

The repugnance with which Thomas describes the male prostitution that follows is shared by Piri, but diluted by the moral imperative of the gang ethic and by a raw hunger for experience:

> I walked up on the roof and breathed in as hard as I could. I wanted to wash my nose out from all the stink. I felt both good and bad. I felt strong and drained. I hadn't liked the scene, but if a guy gotta live, he gotta do it from the bottom of his heart; he has to want it, to feel it.[2]

Years later, long after the gang had ceased to exist as a recognized unit, the same Alfred uses the same street ethic to force Piri to snort heroin, a key episode in his surrender to hard drugs. Piri's subsequent tortured escape from his addiction and his almost religious abhorrence of prison homosexuality illus-

trate, as will be seen below, a progressive shift away from institutionalization, by which he means the abdication of personal
decision making in favor of the blanket norms of a gang, a jail, a
church, or any of the other constructs that limit the freedom of
the individual.

Among the forces militating against individualization are the
stereotypes projected onto racial and ethnic groups in the United
States. Piri's membership in two such groups makes it possible
for Thomas to develop an extraordinarily penetrating critique of
American racism and ethnic prejudice, a critique that draws
ironic overtones from the awkwardness some people feel about
labeling Puerto Ricans.

As a child Piri is confused and hurt by Poppa's evident preference for his sisters and brothers. Only gradually, and at the cost
of great emotional pain, does he come to realize that Poppa,
racially mixed, is projecting his own self-humiliation on the one
child to inherit "bad" features: dark skin and coarse hair. The
other children take after Momma, who is white. Later, when the
family moves into a predominantly Italian neighborhood, Piri
begins to realize that physical features like skin and hair are
used as indices not only to his appearance but to his identity as
well:

> "You okay, kid?" Rocky asked.
> "Yeah," what was left of me said.
> "A-huh," mumbled Big-mouth.
> "He got much heart for a nigger," somebody else said.
> A *spic*, I thought.[3]

In 1944 the family moves to Long Island, where Poppa, anxious for his children to enter the American mainstream, makes a
down payment on a little house in a white middle-class community. Piri is unhappy with the move: "My face tried not to show
resentment at Poppa's decision to leave my streets forever. I felt
that I belonged in Harlem; it was my kind of kick."[4] Nevertheless, Piri tries to adapt to his new setting and even comes to
believe that he has achieved some measure of success. But his
appearance and the influence of black dialect on his speech set
him apart from his "paddy" classmates, and his attempts to

socialize with white girls are rejected. Filled with anger, he leaves home and returns to Harlem on his own. He is sixteen years old.

Some months later Piri and his friend Louie get roughed up and chased by eight paddies as they are coming out of the RKO movie theater on 86th Street. They run from the unequal odds, and one of the paddies yells what he considers the ultimate insult after them:

> "You dirty, fucking shine! I'll get one of you black bastards."
> I screamed back, "Your mammy got fucked by one of us black bastards." *One of us black bastards. Was that me?* I wondered.[5]

The question of racial identity grows more and more pressing for Piri, overshadowing his increasing involvement with drugs and his infatuation for Trina, a girl recently arrived from Puerto Rico. His uncertainty about himself and his inability simply to reject the white racist scheme of values lead to resentment toward his "white" brothers and shame and ambivalence toward his parents. "I felt the shame creep into me. It wasn't right to be ashamed of what one was. It was like hating Momma for the color she was and Poppa for the color he wasn't."[6] Unable to resolve his confusions either in the family or among his friends from El Barrio, he begins hanging around with American blacks. He forms a particularly close, but tense, relationship with Brew, who came from the South just three years ago. The tension springs mostly from Piri's clinging to his identity as a Puerto Rican, thereby putting down Brew, who has no alternative to black:

> I looked at Brew, who was as black as God is supposed to be white. "Man, Brew," I said, "you sure an ugly spook."
> Brew smiled. "Dig this Negro calling out 'spook,'" he said.
> I smiled and said, "I'm a Porty Rican."
> "Ah only sees another Negro in fron' of me," said Brew.[7]

The tension bewtween the youths is generally released through rough horseplay, carefully phrased insults, and Brew's reiterated challenge, "Yuh ain't never been down South." At first Piri ignores the challenge, refusing to accept the idea that the South might be relevant to him. As his friendship with Brew increases, however, he warms to the idea of the trip, partly out of curiosity and partly from a sense of adventure. But before the trip takes place, race and family clash in a decisive confrontation.

Piri's determination to accept himself as black is met with misunderstanding and resentment at home. "'You are not black,' Mamma said, 'you're brown, a nice color, a pretty color.'"[8] Momma, both because she is white and because she is isolated from the English-speaking community, has no problem about race and no real understanding of American racism. It's different with Piri's brother José, who turns on Piri in irrational anger for insisting they are black:

> "I ain't black, damn you! Look at my hair. It's almost blond. My eyes are blue, my nose is straight. My motherfuckin' lips are not like a baboon's ass. My skin is white. White, goddamit! White! Maybe Poppa's a little dark, but that's the Indian blood in him. He's got white blood in him and—"
>
> "So what the fuck am I? Something Poppa an' Momma picked out of the garbage dump?"[9]

The conversation leads to a fight, which in turn releases a flood of destructive feelings through the family and establishes what turns out to be a permanent estrangement between Piri and his brothers. In Poppa, on the other hand, the event, in the context of Piri's imminent departure, produces a rare moment of self revelation and fatherly confidence:

> "I—I got pride in you, *hijo*," he said slowly. "Maybe I—I mean, maybe it looked like I did, or maybe deep down I have. I don't know. Maybe." Poppa's eyes were on his hands, and one fingernail was trying to peel the broken fingernail from another finger. "I ain't got one colored friend," he added, "at least not one American Negro friend. Only dark ones I got are Puerto Ricans or Cubans. I'm not a stupid man. I saw the look of white people on me when I was a young man, when I walked into a place where a dark skin wasn't supposed to be. I noticed how a cold rejection

turned into an indifferent acceptance when they heard my exaggerated accent. I can remember the time when I made my accent heavier, to make me more of a Puerto Rican than the most Puerto Rican there ever was. I wanted a value on me, son."[10]

Poppa's statements confirm what the reader had already begun to understand, that the confrontation between Piri and José is a parody of the Americanization theme prominent in earlier immigrant literatures. For Piri, to become American is to stop being Puerto Rican; but to stop being Puerto Rican is, in the American context, to be black.

When Brew and Piri finally go south, then, with their seamen's papers, the experience is not so much a personal discovery for Piri as a confirmation of what Brew had predicted. The most unexpected experience of the trip is a conversation with Gerald Andrew West, a very light mulatto ("one eighth Negro") from Pennsylvania who is writing a book about the Negro problem in the South—or his perception of that problem:

> "I want to capture on paper the richness of their poverty and their belief in living. I want the words I write to blend with the emotions of their really fantastic ability to endure and absorb the anguish of past memories of the slavery that was the lot of their grandparents. I want to write that despite their burdens they are working with the white man toward a productive relationship."[11]

From this satiric beginning, recorded largely from Brew's hostile point of view, West undergoes a subtle transformation; he proposes a theory of racial options which, though unreal and socially irrelevant, is in an absolute sense more reasonable than the system of restraints and impositions that actually governs this nitty-gritty world of dead-end streets. The increase in West's self-awareness toward the end of his long monologue is a clue to his changed image:

> "Perhaps I was a bit maudlin in describing what I was looking for in the southern Negro, and this may have set

you against me. But I would like you to know that if, because of genetic interbreeding, I cannot truly identify with white or black, I have the right to identify with whatever race or nationality approximates my emotional feelings and physical characteristics."[12]

The idea that the Gerald Andrew Wests of this world should be free to choose their own racial definition is a humorous putdown of the irrational absolutes of racism.

The decision to have West state this idea is technically correct; Piri, seventeen years old, is still too hung up with his problem to handle it dispassionately. In order to prove something in Galveston, he talks his way into a for-whites-only brothel by passing for (Thomas's expression) Puerto Rican and yells at the prostitute before running out of the place, "Baby, I just want you to know that you got fucked by a nigger, by a black man!"[13] It's a trivial act of adolescent bravado, which illustrates the youthful Piri's recurrent use of sex to hurt or humiliate.

After several years of traveling as a seaman, Piri returns to "Home Sweet Harlem" just in time to be present at Momma's deathbed. Her death precipitates Piri's final rupture with Poppa, ending one of the strongest and most troubling relationships of his early life. Cut loose from his earlier moorings, Piri returns to heroin pushing to support himself, which aggravates his addiction to drugs. He finally overcomes his addiction by going cold turkey. Drug pushing is now crossed off the list of job possibilities, so Piri joins his old friend Little Louie and two ex-cons to form a loosely organized gang for occasional armed robbery. The gang is in some ways a development from the gangs of Piri's youth and a critique of their makeshift values. When Piri shows "heart" by beating up an old man in a used car lot robbery, Thomas is repelled and shares his repulsion with the reader. Piri, back home, is torn between inner shame and the need to play the role required by the gang ethic:

I went into the bathroom and looked at myself in the mirror. I couldn't stand what I saw and I puked. The taste was bad. I wanted to say, "I couldn't help it," but I couldn't;

I wanted to lie, but I wouldn't. I washed and washed, but it was not enough. I made a hard face, a *cara-palo* face, and walked back into the kitchen.[14]

Thomas gains credibility from not trying to make his persona uniformly likable. Piri is frequently mean, vindictive, selfish, cruel. During the criminal period of his life he is pictured as what he is: a low-grade hood. Thomas's books are essentially the story of his climb upward to rejoin the human race.

The big turning point in Piri's life occurs in 1955. He and his associates are robbing a night club when an off-duty cop opens fire on them, hitting Piri in the chest. Piri fires back, gravely wounding the cop. He is captured and rushed to Bellevue Prison Ward. When he has recovered sufficiently, he is taken to the Tombs, tried, and sentenced to a term of five to fifteen years, which he serves at Comstock State Prison.

The last quarter of *Down These Mean Streets* is about the prison experience, which is also the subject of *Seven Long Times*, published in 1974. The use made of the material is quite different in each of these two books. In the first, prison is another chapter in Piri's continued quest for self-discovery; the second focuses on the prison system itself, its cruelty and humor, its flaws and possibilities. This book contains a vivid description of the Comstock prison riot of August 1955 and helps explain some of the conditions that led to that riot and to the riots at Attica in 1971 and at Santa Fe in 1980.

On an autobiographical level both books are about Piri's "rehabilitation," a term Thomas uses with self-conscious irony. For Piri, rehabilitation means resisting the pressures of what he sees as a morally and intellectually destructive penal system. His determination *"They ain't gonna break me"*[15] becomes the theme of his seven years at Comstock. And this theme gives continuity to Thomas's work, because "they," the forces threatening to break Piri in prison, are much the same as the temptations to which he had been yielding most of his life in the world outside. One of these temptations is institutionalization, which Thomas describes in the case of a young con who has just been returned to prison after some time on parole:

He was glad to be back. He was home with his familiar buddy-con faces, his father images in the persons of both hacks and cons. Home where his brothers were. He was back where he didn't have to worry about looking for a job or hassling income tax forms, where he didn't have to compete to the extent demanded on the outside. He was home where he would be fed, clothed, and watched over, where he wouldn't have to make any real decisions. Home again![16]

Sex is another institutional trap. No one has described better than Thomas the indignity, sadism, pain, and grotesque attraction of prison sex in all its forms, from rape to "marriage." Throughout his prison term Piri is subject to homosexual overtures, and at times he is hard put to live up to his early boast, "I came in here my father's son and I'll be damned if I go out my mother's daughter."[17] External pressures of threats and bribes and the internal need for some form of sexual expression are constantly operating to break down his resistence. Piri wins out, partly because he fears homosexuality as a violation of his sexual integrity, partly because he sees it as a potential crack in the wall of his defense against the system:

> ...I ain't gonna break. One time. That's all I have to do it. Just one time and it's gone time. I'll be screwing faggots as fast as I can get them. I'm not gonna get institutionalized. I don't want to lose my hatred of this damn place. Once you lose your hatred, then the can's got you.[18]

The racial tensions that used to tear Piri apart become more manageable in prison. Not that racial tensions aren't in evidence: on the contrary, Comstock is impregnated with racism, with the guards, trustees, and Caucasian prisoners constituting a sort of metasociety of privileged separation. But for Piri the *personal* strain gradually lessens as he learns to approach situations with greater objectivity and discrimination. For example, the broad category of "paddy" gives way to an appreciation of individual differences; many of the prison whites are bigots, but some are not: the understanding chaplain; Johnny Lee, who plays hand-

ball with blacks and takes a beating from the other white cons
for not maintaining standards; the two very decent cops who
take Piri from Comstock to the Bronx to face warrants still pend-
ing against him. And in Comstock Piri seems less troubled by
the identity question; most of the Puerto Rican prisoners are
racially mixed and all are subsumed, with American blacks, under
the designation "niggers." The decision was made for him. Even
more important, Piri learns to distinguish between membership
in a given racial group and bigotry, which has no racial boundaries. He becomes a member of the Black Muslims for a while,
but what he takes from them is a far cry from their characteristic
militancy:

> I learned many things, because it involved me. I became
> curious about everything human. Though I didn't remain a
> muslim after my eventual release from the big jail, I never
> forgot one thing that Muhammad said, for I believed it too:
> "No matter what a man's color or race he has a need of
> dignity and he'll go anywhere, become anything, or do
> anything to get it—anything..."[19]

As his hangup with racial identification lessens, Piri begins thinking in terms of the essential sameness of all human beings under
their accidental physical or cultural differences: "The soul and
spirit is blood with blue eyes, dark skin, and curly hair."[20] Piri
still has a lot of bigotry to face after he leaves prison, but his civil
war is, except for a few skirmishes, over.

Another change that takes place in Piri is his attitude toward
his imprisonment. During his first years at Comstock he sees his
sentence as an isolated happening, as arbitary as the crime which
preceded it. "The reasoning that my punishment was deserved
was absent. As prison blocks off your body, so it suffocates your
mind."[21] As time passes, the apparent arbitrariness shapes itself
into causal patterns. His punishment is linked to his crimes, and
these are seen as having their genesis within the very society to
which they were directed:

> I committed the crime, I pulled those stickups. I'd stand up
> to that. But who's going to stand up and admit it was this

country's racial and economic inequalities that forced so many of us to the brink of insanity, making our anger and frustration so great that we literally blew ourselves over the precipice into deep, dark whirlpools of drugs and crime?[22]

Piri never complains that his punishment is undeserved. He admits the criminal's obligation to pay a "debt" to society and he recognizes society's right to demand rehabilitation as a condition of restored freedom. He vehemently criticizes, however, the vindictive, sadistic, counterproductive treatment to which inmates of American prisons are too often subjected. Appendix 1 of *Seven Long Times* is a compassionate and intelligent critique of the nation's prison and parole systems. It would be an excellent basis for a required training program for all prison directors and employees.

Appendix 1 was written twenty-four years after Thomas began serving his sentence; it evidences mental and emotional maturity that are not yet characteristic of the Piri who is paroled in October 1955. Although he has made remarkable progress in self-understanding and both formal and informal education, Piri returns to a free life under the burden of nine years' parole and three years' probation for armed robberies in the Bronx. He is returned, jobless, to the drug-ridden streets that led him into crime, and now he has the handicap of a prison record in addition to that of race. The story of his succeeding struggles and his hard-won strengths is the subject matter of the third—and most impressive—volume of his autobiography.

Down These Mean Streets is about sin, *Seven Long Times* is about penance, and *Savior, Savior, Hold My Hand*, structured on religious institutions, is about varieties of personal salvation. It begins when Piri returns to live with his aunt in El Barrio, where his precarious freedom will depend on his having the "heart" to resist, day after day, the familiar streets, the old friends, the easy money. The bricklaying trade he learned in prison proves useless, because his race and his criminal record bar him from the union. He gets a menial job in a clothing factory, then in a bakery, and supplements these by running an elevator three nights a week. The practical details of daily living, however, soon recede before the parallel concerns that come to dominate the book: Piri's marriage and family life and his involvement with church groups.

Nita, the girl Piri marries, is a member of his aunt's Puerto Rican Pentecostal church. The time devoted in *Savior, Savior, Hold My Hand* to courtship, marriage, and fatherhood establishes Piri's maturing capacity for responsiblity, altruism, and love as a necessary condition for his growing sense of social mission. Particularly touching is the chapter on the wedding night, in which Piri tries to exorcize, through Nita, the horror of his prison memories. The recurrent motif *I am not an animal* and Piri's tenderness in coupling with his virgin bride contrast significantly with the crudity and even cruelty of his youthful sex acts.

The family theme expands when Nita gives birth to a son. Piri, ironically repeating his own father's mistake, moves his family to the grass and trees and white picket fences of a small Long Island community. Eyebrows are again raised at his color, but the snubbings and innuendos have little effect on Piri now. His satisfaction with his job and family gives him enough personal security to ignore the sporadic barks of prejudice. When he decides to move back to the city to be closer to his work, however, his attempt to sell his property to an American black, a minister, brings down on him the full impact of community racism. The Better Civic Improvement Committee blocks the sale, the house is vandalized, and Piri eventually loses it under the weight of violations slapped on it by the township. Thus ends the attempt to mold Piri, Nita, and their son into a typical suburban American family.

The second major theme of the book, institutional Christianity, is introduced when *Tía* tries to explain to her nephew what it means to her to be a Pentecostal:

> "It's what binds much of us poor Puertorriquenos together. It gives us strength to live in these conditions. It's like being part of a *familia* that is together in Christo and we help each other with the little materials we may possess."[23]

Piri, wanting badly to be "part of a *familia*" again and searching for positive influences to keep him straight, begins to attend services at the aunt's Spanish Mission Pentecostal Church, where he meets Nita. He comes to accept Christ as his personal savior and even to testify at street-corner meetings. The story of his conversion comes to the attention of the American Bible Society, which sends one of its writers to do a tract on him. Through this writer he comes to meet John Clause, another ex-convict convert who runs a church-supported club working with Harlem youth. Realizing Piri's potential usefulness in this work, Clause invites him to leave his bakery job and work full time for the club. Piri, now in his early thirties, accepts.

It would be interesting to have Clause's account of the progressively deteriorating relationship between Piri and himself. There is no reason to doubt that Thomas wanted to give a scrupulously honest description of the relationship, but his portrayal of Clause is too close to monsterhood to be easily credible. It is hard, in fact, to see how either man's perceptions of the other could be objective. They were too much alike: ex-cons, converts, competitors for the recognition that comes of doing the Lord's work well. In one respect they were too different: Clause was a paddy.

According to Piri's account of his work at the club, Clause soon begins to use him by taking credit for his success with the black and Puerto Rican youngsters who relate to him so easily and who mistrust Clause almost instinctively. This leads to a mounting resentment on Piri's part and an increasing disinclination to follow Clause's orders and suggestions, which are based on legality when Piri's leanings are toward mercy. Eventually Piri quits, and Clause, with calculated vengefulness, tries to frame him and have him sent back to prison for parole violation. By that time, however, Piri's work in the community is well known, and the charge against him—possession of some zip guns which he had taken away from an emotionally disturbed member of a street gang—is dismissed.

The hostility between Piri and John Clause is symptomatic of what Thomas sees as a fundamental sociological and cultural conflict between his people—the blacks and Puerto Ricans living in "our calles"—and the white establishment. The conflict is explicitly stated in terms of religious organizations: Tia's Pentecostal church is clearly part of El Barrio, in contrast to the unidentified church group supporting John Clause and to the "Great Church downtown" which offered to let the members of Clause's club use its Sunday school facilities. What happens at this church and Piri's reaction to what happens are at the heart of Thomas's thinking. At first the Sunday school sessions go well, but gradually the regular parishioners begin to show, in mild enough ways, disapproval of their guests' increasing boisterousness. Piri is outraged, and if his attitude seems unreasonable, it is because we have missed the point he is making: the black-Puerto Rican minority must be accepted in terms of its own values, its own code. To clothe religion in the garments of any sort of cultural absolutism is not acceptable:

> It was like we weren't equals. It was as if they were the chosen ones—despite the teachings in their Bibles—like they were sent to save us by getting us a hearing with Christ. But like it had to be on their own terms.[24]

By "their own terms" Piri means the imposition of WASP sociocultural standards, a practice long associated with Protestant missionary work in colonial settings, as when the missionaries dressed Hawaian women in Mother Hubbards. Numerous verbal references show that Thomas had this colonial mission analogy explicitly in mind:

> In the Bible it says that Christians are supposed to spread the word, but God Almighty, I think they at least should try understanding the people they're spreading the word to.[25]
>
> ...here in our Barrio, we're tired of being pressured by all kinds of half-ass white rulers.[26]
>
> "We got some missionaries to El Barrio who wheel and deal in souls because they know so many of us want to believe in something other than this hell we're living in."[27]

Attempts to convert the culture of El Barrio into the typical American way of life are, for Piri Thomas, a sort of internal colonialism.

This is getting to the nitty-gritty (a favorite word of Piri's) of tolerance for ethnic and cultural diversity. How elastic is tolerance? The members of Piri's club, though sometimes presented with the cuteness of Dead End Kids, are filled with barely controlled hostility, which often breaks out in extreme violence, even murder. They make little effort to modify or restrict language and behavior patterns that they know are offensive to others. (Someone scribbles on the door of the club, "Dear Lord, we were only trying to communicate when we say motherfucker....Amen."[28]) Yet Piri bristles at attempts by "outsiders" to modify these patterns. To be fair, he deplores the violence and works hard to control it or channel it into less destructive outlets. But there remains a broad area of behavior that he finds acceptable, part of the individual or community lifestyle, which most Americans would find rude, aggressive, and antisocial. His awareness of this fact and of the challenge it presents to the contemporary American social thought is one of Thomas's major insights.

The book ends with a perceptible distancing between Nita and Piri over the latter's increasing skepticism about not only specific institutions but the relevance of Christianity itself to the world of El Barrio:

> "I know Christ is great, honey. I just wish he'd come down and walk with us nitty-gritty. Baby, I'm not putting God down. I'm just wondering why the hell we've allowed certain people to put us down. How the hell can I listen to the words of Christ and how He carried the cross? I can't carry no cross and be nailed to it at the same damned time. Wow, honey, don't you dig that to us people of the Barrio the ghetto is our church, and the only way we're gonna make a heaven out of this hell is by getting together. Jesus, honey, ain't I right?"[29]

This and the two-edged assertion "We're gonna walk tall or not at all, World" remain Thomas's final statement. *Stories from El Barrio*, published by Knopf in 1978, is aimed at younger readers and adds little to the intellectual thrust of his first three books.

The quotations included throughout this chapter illustrate the features of Thomas's style, which is at its most characteristic in strong, linguistically inventive dialogue based on Harlem street language and enlivened, in the speech of bilinguals, with unexpected interjections of Spanish words and phrases. It has a great deal of verisimilitude, as if just transcribed from a field tape. This apparent naturalness is a considerable achievement, for Thomas's dialogue is, perhaps more than most writers', carefully contrived and individualized. One can read almost almost any page of Thomas's work and recognize immediately who wrote it. The dialogue has a style and distinctiveness that is seldom, if ever, found in real conversation.

Even the juxtapositioning of Spanish and English vocabulary, a practice of many Nuyorican speakers, is stylized in Thomas. Sue Klau, in an excellent analysis of Thomas's language, consulted a group of Nuyoricans who were Thomas's contemporaries in El Barrio to check on the authenticity of his usage. "Basically, the ten sources agreed that Piri Thomas's Spanish/English patterns are representative but not always authentic. They said that Spanish and English words *are* combined by members of the New Breed [Nuyoricans], but not always the way Piri combines them in his writings."[30]

Thomas has created a style of his own, which has become a hallmark of his work. But he writes well in other styles and registers, too. He has a real flair for representing black speech and for mimicking middle-class whites. Through subtle word choices he makes John Clause actually *sound* insincere. His expository and descriptive passages are written in good standard English, and he occasionally throws in a stunningly beautiful line: "How put into words the ugliness and beauty of street life and a boy's constant wants?"[31]

Thomas's basic, most personal style, however, is the street dialogue described above, and this is a limitation, especially in his later works. The "Piri" style is fine for capturing the responses of *Down These Mean Streets*, but it becomes a hindrance in reporting Piri's greater maturity, reflectiveness, and insight in *Savior, Savior, Hold My Hand*. This self-imposed limitation is strange, considering the range of language resources that Thomas has at his command. It is as if, by demanding the readers' acceptance of *his* style, Thomas is underscoring his demand for the acceptance of a way of life to which, flawed and limited as it may be, he has laid a personal claim.

No matter how one reacts to the style, the substance of Thomas's work is of permanent interest. Others have added to but no one has surpassed his assessment of the Nuyorican experience.

NOTES

1. Piri Thomas, *Down These Mean Streets*, p. 62.
2. Ibid., pp. 68-69.
3. Ibid., p. 41.
4. Ibid., p. 86.
5. Ibid., p. 121.
6. Ibid., p. 122.
7. Ibid., p. 123.
8. Ibid., p. 135.
9. Ibid., p. 144.
10. Ibid., p. 152.
11. Ibid., pp. 168-69.
12. Ibid., p. 174.
13. Ibid., p. 185.
14. Ibid., p. 214.
15. Ibid., p. 240.
16. Piri Thomas, *Seven Long Times*, p. 98.
17. Ibid., p. 67.
18. *Mean Streets*, pp. 251-52.
19. Ibid., p. 283.
20. Ibid., pp. 284-85.
21. Ibid., p. 245.
22. *Seven Long Times*, p. 220.
23. Piri Thomas, *Savior, Savior, Hold My Hand*, p. 20.
24. Ibid., p. 257.
25. Ibid., p. 315.
26. Ibid., p. 319.
27. Ibid., p. 360.
28. Ibid., p. 287.
29. Ibid., p. 360.
30. Sue Klau, "The Use of Spanish and the Works of Piri Thomas," p. 27.
31. *Savior*, p. 94.

4

BARRIO LIVES

The critical and popular recognition awarded *Down These Mean Streets* has tended to distract attention from a number of similar books published from the late 1960s on. One can almost speak in terms of a literary subgenre defined as a narrative, possibly autobiographical, about a Puerto Rican male growing up in El Barrio and coming to grips with poverty, discrimination, gang warfare, drugs, crime, and sometimes imprisonment. These experiences have been common enough in New York's Hispanic neighborhoods certainly, but the regularity with which they appear in this literature suggests a selection process at work. The example of Claude Brown's *Manchild in the Promised Land* some years earlier must have alerted publishers to the potential market for books written about ghetto life from the inside.[1] And the inside view with most market appeal was one that looked on scenes far removed from middle-class comfort and sobriety.

It might be expected that books belonging to this subgenre are imitative and repetitious. This is only partly true. Types of experience are repeated, but specific incidents are handled distinctively. Individual responses to the same situations vary, as do emphases, goals, and self-images. Most important, each protagonist is uniquely characterized. Some idea of the individualization possible within a narrow range of material can be seen in a comparison of five books of the class just described.

Manuel Manrique's *Island in Harlem* deals with a quest for manhood in the morally self-contained world of El Barrio. The plot centers on the enmity between Antonio, a black Puerto

Rican dishwasher recently arrived from the Island, and Feli, an intensely proud white Puerto Rican gang leader. The enmity develops over Antonio's ingenuous and superficial attraction toward Feli's girl Lilliam, a black from Alabama. The realistic, convincing development of these three characters and their interrelationships is well handled in terms of both conscious and subconscious complexities. The love-fear attraction between Feli and Lilliam, for example, overlies unspoken racial attitudes:

> They made love with the same passion as always and with more hidden thought than ever before, at least on Lilliam's part. Feli, as always, could vaguely feel, "I'm white; do you realize that, you little mulatto?" and she could more consciously assert, "I'm from Alabama; you're a spick," and both could say aloud, "I love you."[2]

Feli's ambiguous but strong feeling for Lilliam and the racial heterogeneity of his gang restrain him from overtly expressing his racism, but it flashes out in the contempt he feels for "the dishwasher" and in the irrational pitch of his anger when he sees Lilliam and Antonio dancing:

> Feli's eyes, burning like an eagle's descending on its prey, finally caught Lilliam and Tony. His white skin—his secret pride among his mulatto and Negro friends—tautened with the shiver of a panther's before it springs.
> "There they are!" he said. He looked with disgust at Antonio's dark skin.[3]

Intuition about the racial substratum of Feli's antagonism sharpens Antonio's awareness of race, but there is only one occasion (he is refused service at a store in a racially tense neighborhood) when he is rejected because of his color by someone other than Feli. On the other hand, there are several situations in which his color seems to lend him a special sexual attraction. Once he is drawn into bizarre sexual practices by a white Greenwich Village couple excited by the contrast between his skin and the woman's. And his homosexual boss, a very well-drawn minor character, is swollen with tenderness and lust at the sight of the dishwasher's dark, sweaty torso.

In terms of personal and social identity, however, the racial theme is not explored very far. In one scene Antonio feels impelled to join a crowd of freedom-marching blacks battling the police:

> And he rushed out into St. Nicholas Avenue to fight the police like the others. He was in the middle of the street, in the middle of a crowd of American Negroes, fighting like them. And for the first time in his life he—a Puerto Rican—felt glad that he was a Negro and an American. "But am I really an American? I'm black—no doubt about that. But an American?"[4]

This somewhat forced and uncertain identification with American blacks is an interesting theme, but in this book it leads nowhere. Antonio's color is, in reference to the plot, juxtaposed only against Feli's, another Puerto Rican's. He has no choice of his private field of combat: it is, unalterably, Spanish Harlem.

The basic weakness of *Island in Harlem* is that so much of Antonio's energy leads nowhere. The book is about his attempts to achieve, in an unfamiliar world, a sense of manhood that he finds personally satisfying. But his quest is constantly blocked by confusion, naiveté, and an ill-digested machismo that produces false reactions and pointless gestures. His early love for his distant cousin Margarita is muddled by his sudden attraction for Lilliam and a number of lackadaisical sexual encounters. As a form of revenge against Feli for the latter's threat against Margarita, Antonio plans to rape Lilliam, but she defuses all his resolve by offering to surrender herself willingly. And the code of honor and humiliation understood, presumably, by Antonio and Feli in their last fight is so subtle and so highly ritualized that even the members of Feli's gang fail to recognize it. At the end of the book Antonio, with a painful bullet wound in the shoulder, is climbing the stairs to Margarita's apartment:

> Feli and the Emperors seemed now a distant memory; but they were still there, and in the jungle of the Barrio there were others like them.
> But a man had to go on as if he were going to live forever.[5]

Nothing is resolved here, nothing achieved. Perhaps that is what Manuel Manrique wants to say about Spainish Harlem.

Uncertainty and lack of resolution also characterize the ending of Lefty Barreto's *Nobody's Hero*, in which Manni, Barreto's protagonist, leaves prison to return to the drug- and crime-paved streets that led him there. In a foreword to his book, Barreto acknowledges Piri Thomas's influence, which is evident in style, attitudes, and sometimes even vocabulary. For example, Manni's resistence to prison institutionalization is uncomfortably similar to Piri's treatment of the subject, discussed in chapter 3:

> And yet I resisted, knowing that my one chance was to reject the whole miserable thing. Refusing to be institutionalized because I had seen what institutionalization did to a man. He got used to living this way, by the whistle and by the club. Afraid of responsibility. Afraid to try. So I have wanted to hate every second of it. Hate it and survive.[6]

Manni's comments on prison homosexuality are also reminiscent of Piri's, and Piri's efforts toward self-education behind bars are probably the model for Manni's curiously gratuitous references to his prison reading, including what is surely one of the funniest lines in prison literature: "Late that afternoon, as I lay on my bunk reading Camus, five inmates appeared at my bedside."[7]

The importance of these influences should not be exaggerated, however; Manni is not just an imitation Piri. His early home life and his relationship to other members of the family seem much less stable than Piri's; in fact, it is his mother's complaint against him for stealing her radio that first sends Manni to prison. Because of this lack of emotional security at home, Manni's social and psychological dependence on street gangs is more intense and longer lasting than Piri's. Barreto is expecially good at contrasting the real viciousness of gang behavior with the movie and comic-book fantasies that are its nutrients:

> The motorcycle jackets that were the thing in the early fifties had been replaced by black capes à la Dracula and the three-quarter raincoat. I didn't take to the cape too

tough, but I dug my bad shiny raincoat and my bamboo cane.[8]

Like so many other issues in this book, the question of Puerto Rican-black relations is defined in a gang context. Although Manni describes himself as *trigueño*—racially mixed—he doesn't identify with American blacks, perhaps because his identity is stabilized by the memory of his childhood in Puerto Rico. As leader of the Sportsmen, a sort of gang federation with both black and Puerto Rican components, Manni tries to maintain an *e pluribus unum* policy to minimize intergroup tensions, but his philosophy is clearly of the separate-but-equal variety:

> The cat explained to me that the black Sportsmen were coming around and rumbling with the Forsyth Boys on the sneak. And they called names like spic and shit. But I was taken by surprise because the blacks were always saying that black and Puerto Rican were the same thing. In a way I resented that, because I knew this wasn't true. We were both underdogs, but the Puerto Ricans were as different from the blacks as the blacks were different from the whites. We had our own culture too.[9]

The tenuous coexistence between the black and Puerto Rican groups ends in an outbreak of violence in which a young black girl is killed. Soon afterwards Manni, losing heart in gang life and conscious of his waning leadership among his younger and more aggressive companions, allows himself to be eased out of the presidency of the Sportsmen.

The second half of *Nobody's Hero* describes Manni's protracted struggle with heroin addiction and his imprisonment for theft. Other elements of the narrative—the woman Manni moved in with, his job on a delivery truck—are properly subordinated to the dominating drug experience, which is sometimes detailed with crude force, sometimes with poetic sensitivity: "And that's all it took, a grain. Like the atom, that one grain had the power to set off a chain reaction that veered the course of my life."[10] Barreto also gives a good feeling for the problem's social dimensions, showing how it destroys interpersonal relationships and sits like an almost visible plague on the neighborhood: "teen-agers bopping by, and old dazed winos on the dirty stoop look-ing at nothing and rapping to no one. The buildings themselves seem to be nodding, bent with age and corrosion."[11]

Although there are good moments in *Nobody's Hero*, the book as a whole suffers from poor judgment and insufficient editing. Barreto often fails to distinguish between his characters' inter-ests and his readers'. For example, we are expected, in the gang section, to endow adolescent posturings and rituals with a mean-ingfulness that for most adults they do not have. Consequently, long passages, sometimes whole chapters, seem prolix, repeti-tious, trivial.

Another flaw is the frequent strain on credibility. When the book opens, Manni, eleven years old, is seduced in the woods by a nineteen year-old college girl, sister of one of the matrons at a camp Manni is attending for children with a family history of tuberculosis. The girl is not a nymphomaniac or anything like that; she's a very nice girl with a genuine sympathy for the minority group kids at the camp. Whether or not such a girl *might* have carried out a seduction of that sort—even as an ex-pression of youthful liberalism—the improbability is so great that, added to other improbabilities and inconsistencies, it weakens the book's verisimilitude.

Another book that makes strong demands on the reader's willingness to suspend disbelief is Nick Cruz's autobiography *Run Baby Run*, "written with Jamie Buckingham." This is a St. Paul-type conversion story, popular among Christians through-out the ages. The first half of the book covers Nick's unloved, rebellious childhood in Puerto Rico and his subsequent gang life in New York, where he is sent at the age of fifteen because his parents can no longer control him. The second half begins with his conversion by David Wilkerson and his eventual training and church ministry.

To emphasize the Lord's power to soften even the hardest of hearts, the authors present the unregenerate Nicky as the mean-est, most hate-filled of gang leaders and his Mau-Maus as the most vicious of gangs. Scenes of violence and sadism go well beyond similar scenes elsewhere:

Before the boy could move, the two boys yanked his arms straight out from his body, spread eagle. Moving so fast you could hardly follow his hand, Carlos brought the knife up in a fast, vicious thrust and jabbed it almost to the hilt into the child's armpit. The boy jerked and screamed in pain. The blood gushed out and quickly flooded his white shirt with a crimson red.

Pulling the knife out of the boy's flesh, he flipped it into his other hand. "See man," he leered viciously, thrusting the knife upward again into the other armpit, "I'm left handed too."[12]

The violence, unfortunately, is more persuasive than Nicky's easy passage to the simple piety of biblical Christianity. This is not exactly a failure of credibility, for we know that Nicky Cruz the author, who once lived by the codes of the street, did change his life and become a successful preacher. But the motivations for that change are not adequately developed in the book. Wilkerson's repeated assurance that "Jesus loves you, Nicky" does not satisfy the mind's demand for a stimulus compelling enough to effect so radical a conversion. The faithful will accept divine grace as an explanation, but faith is not literature.

Several other things in *Run Baby Run* raise doubts about its objectivity. Nicky, who comes late to the New York scene, gains prominence and leadership in the gang so rapidly that he soon appears as a superhero, a street-epic star whose fame spreads like that of Hector or Achilles—or Superman. Nicky the writer doesn't make enough effort to achieve an adult perspective on his youthful protagonist. Toward the end of the book, when Nicky is a practicing evangelist, the portrayal becomes more believable, although even here Nicky seems a bit wiser and less fallible than most human beings get a chance to become.

Nicky's picture of Puerto Rico, where he grew up, reads like a collage of impressions drawn from third-rate horror films with tropical settings: "At night the sounds of the voodoo drums roll down from the palm-covered mountains as the witch doctors practice their trade—offering sacrifices and dancing with snakes in the light of flickering fires."[13] Snakes are so rare in Puerto Rico that finding one usually merits press coverage; palms are sea-level trees; voodoo and witch doctor are terms used for Haitian religious practices, not Puerto Rican. Inaccuracies as gross as those in Nicky's description suggest an immense carelessness, if not downright dishonesty.

Nicky's language proficiencies are also confusing. When preaching, he uses an interpreter to translate his Spanish into English; yet, he insists on speaking to a young Puerto Rican couple, Israel and Rosa, in English, a language that Rosa doesn't understand and that Israel has to translate for her. [14]

Despite these weaknesses, *Run Baby Run* has enjoyed a long publication history since it first came out in 1968. A good part of its popularity can be explained by its church sponsorship and by the exposure that Nicky Cruz has enjoyed as an evangelist preacher. But there is an additional appeal in the book's being a double success story: Nicky escapes both a life of sin and life in El Barrio. And one life is an objective correlative of the other.

The view of El Barrio as a place not to love but to leave can also be found in Humberto Cintrón's *Frankie Cristo*, a short book that deserves to be better known, especially for its sharp, realistic dialogue. This book describes the same sort of street fighting, addiction, and crime as the others, but is distinguished by a theme that relates it more closely to the literatures of earlier immigrant groups: the protagonist's final determination to enter the American mainstream through the door of higher education. This determination is dramatized through the pregnancy of Frankie's girl Regina. According to Barrio and family codes this accident should result in a teenage marriage and a lifetime of low-paying jobs and nagging discontent. Frankie, not without compunction, opts for a different future. He persuades Regina to have an abortion and he joins the navy—a significant act in itself—where he plans to finish high school in order to qualify for later study under the G.I. Bill. The outward movement into a more open world is caught nicely in the rhythm of the final paragraph:

> The day slipped by quickly. Frankie filled out forms, answered questions, was examined, poked, pulled, jabbed, squeezed, injected—and finally, head erect, right hand raised, he swore allegiance and was herded into a busload of re-

cruits and hauled out of Manhattan, taking a tunnel at
Canal Street, emerging in Jersey City across the Hudson
River, and turning south. Frankie, looking out the win-
dow, caught a glimpse of the jagged gray silhouette of
Manhattan... then was lost in the monotony of Americana
on a highway heading far away from 109th Street.[15]

To be "lost in the monotony of Americana" is obviously not
the best of all possible conditions, but it does suggest, in context, a positive adaptation readily understood by millions of
Americans whose parents or grandparents left other ghettos in
search of a better life for themselves or their children. Many of
today's Nuyorican writers and intellectuals, on the other hand,
nurtured on protest poetry and ethnic rights, may read that final
sentence as critical of Frankie's assimilationism. Humberto Cintrón
himself, after going to California for an MA in urban studies,
returned to El Barrio to work with the Community News Service, helping the American dream grow in ethnic soil.

But many ordinary, nonintellectual Nuyoricans (or ex-Nuyoricans)
want to cut their ethnic roots and leave them to shrivel away
among the old associations. In a report for the New York Times
News Service Richard Severo describes this group:

As the Puerto Ricans give every indication of wanting to
relate to the dominant white society, there appears to be a
deep and widening rift in New York City between working, upwardly mobile Puerto Ricans and the large numbers
of chronically indigent neighbors they left behind in the
South Bronx and East Harlem.[16]

While it may be a real and increasingly prominent facet of the
Nuyorican experience, successful adaptation to middle-class life
in the United States has not been a widespread theme in Nuyorican
letters. It may become more widespread as more and more people cross the invisible class line into Westchester and the better
sections of Long Island, but it will never be a real community
theme for the simple reason that its heroes have left the community. And from a market viewpoint, adaptation does not pos-
sess the dramatic possibilities of struggle. There is one book,

however, where Americanization is so openly embraced and the psychology of upward mobility so nakedly revealed that it is well worth reading, despite its minimal literary pretensions. The book is Richard Ruiz's short, bitter family memoir, *The Hungry American*.

Born into the harsh poverty of rural Puerto Rico during the depression, Ruiz tells of seeing his first indoor toilet when the family rents an apartment in "the first project built in Mayaguez for the poor with Washington money."[17] When he is twelve years old, he is sent to join his parents in their new home on East 110th Street, where he is struck by the dirty, rundown condition of the building and the neighborhood. Some years later, in a pitiful effort to improve their lot, they move to 106th Street, which is still inhabited by a few Jewish and Italian families:

> Unquestionably, these people weren't too enthusiastic about the Puerto Ricans moving into their block. The expression on their faces was one of intense feeling of animosity: their frustration and resignation was unconcealable, and in a few months they all packed up their belongings and fled. It was a pitiful sight to see the adverse transition of a fairly good neighborhood. The quiet, hard-working inhabitants were gradually replaced by loud, shiftless and scanty-minded elements. The once predominantly quiet atmosphere faded away in the presence of the loud sound of Spanish music from the high-tuned record players; the well-mannered groups, that once assembled on the sidewalk during the hot summer months, were soon replaced by hoodlums with little respect for anybody or anything. In short, these newcomers brought about the downfall of a fairly good neighborhood and, unfortunately, I was a member of that destructive force.[18]

The desire to dissociate himself from the Puerto Rican community is evident throughout Ruiz's book and is psychologically related to the cleavage between Ruiz and other members of his immediate family. The appalling nightmare of family relationships, which is the real subject of *The Hungry American*, parallels and perhaps determines the author's broader social relations. After his marriage, a move to Newark, and the birth of his first child, Ruiz's attachment to his adopted land becomes more explicit:

> But as time passed, my role in society began to change. I set out to search for the good old American dream. My Puerto Rican heritage was no longer appealing to me. I wanted to blend into society. I was Americanizing myself more and more until it became virtually an article of faith with me that I had to strike a deliberate contrast with what has been called the "Puerto Rican way of life." Gradually my love for Puerto Rico ebbed while my admiration for America rose.[19]

Ruiz records no instances of social discrimination against him. His name is never held against him, and he finds that "show the people you have knowledge, respect and dignity and chances are they will by-pass the color of your skin."[20] In his brief participation in Newark politics Ruiz disappoints the professionals by refusing to help exploit ethnic loyalties: "I felt we were Americans, and as Americans our responsiblity was to work collectively for the betterment of all residents of Newark. Not just the Puerto Ricans."[21]

Ruiz's optimism about the United States is not born of an easy or protected life there. In addition to his constant family conflicts, he writes of frequent unemployment and other disappointments. But he always sees new hope, another opportunity waiting for the person willing to grasp it. In an afterword to the memoir he mentions the generally prosperous adaptation of different members of the Ruiz family in Manhattan, Long Island, West Virginia, Florida, Arizona, and California. One brother is a police lieutenant, another an accountant; one sister is married to an accountant, the other to an engineer. It's an impressive achievement for a first generation. *The Hungry American* is a naive book in many ways; a lot of people would find its social attitudes shallow and jingoistic. But it is an honest book and undoubtedly reflects the sentiments and aspirations of large numbers of Puerto Ricans passing through New York to other parts of the new land.

Most of the books discussed above, and others like them, are out of print, ephemeral jetsam left behind by the tide of American publishing. Some were privately printed, others were picked up by publishers hoping to exploit a rising interest in minority life and ghetto violence. None has great literary value. But they are honest books, and their interest lies in their statements and judgments on life in El Barrio. The judgments are not optimistic. Manrique and Barreto leave their heroes in El Barrio facing lives of little hpes bound to be defeated in the cyclical pattern of community frustration. Cruz, Cintrón, and Ruiz see salvation in escape from the community and its mores.

The following chapters will deal with writers who share a more optimistic perception of the Nuyorican community. In this perception the community is dynamic, capable of evolution through changes in the feelings and desires of the people who live there. In its belief in the possibility of betterment, this is a perception of the American dream projected in unfamiliar images.

NOTES

1. There are many similarities between Brown's book and Piri Thomas's *Mean Streets*, but Thomas had not read *Manchild* at the time he wrote his book. See "Dialogue with Piri Thomas," *The Rican: A Journal of Contemporary Puerto Rican Thought*," 2 (Winter 1972): 21.
2. Manuel Manrique, *Island in Harlem*, p. 200.
3. Ibid., p. 63.
4. Ibid., p. 196
5. Ibid., p. 223.
6. Lefty Barreto, *Nobody's Hero*, p. 248.
7. Ibid., p. 237.
8. Ibid., p. 103.
9. Ibid., p. 110.
10. Ibid., p. 132.
11. Ibid., p. 191.
12. Nicky Cruz, *Run Baby Run*, p. 55.
13. Ibid., p. 17.
14. Ibid., pp. 228, 236.
15. Humberto Cintrón, *Frankie Cristo*, p. 107.
16. Richard Severo, "Faces of Change—Seeking Good Life in N.Y.," *San Juan Star*, 23 November 1977, p. 24.
17. Richard Ruiz, *The Hungry American*, p. 4.
18. Ibid., p. 38.
19. Ibid., p. 55.
20. Ibid.
21. Ibid., p.61.

5
A WOMAN'S PERSPECTIVE

Nicholasa Mohr, whose surname is identical to the present writer's only by mere coincidence, is the first Nuyorican writer to combine formal experimentation with a vision of a community that has been evolving over a period of thirty years or more, from her childhood memories of the early 1940s to the maturing adaptations of just yesterday. It is reassuring to turn from the violence-oriented narratives of her male contemporaries to her more familiar world of home and school and of people who try to be decent and succeed more often than not. Ironically, the strengths of her books were at first a disappointment to publishers, who urged her to falsify her vision in exchange for a stall at the market-place. When she submitted her first book of stories to a publishing house,

> the editor suggested that he was really looking for something "more authentic," something that describes what *really* goes on in El Barrio. Someone along the lines of a female Piri Thomas—drugs, rape, crime, prostitution, the whole chilling spectacle of ghetto existence. That's what most readers seem to want. . . . [1]

Mohr's dramatization of the belief that Puerto Ricans can and often do find a place in the New York sun finds little favor among those who prefer to see El Barrio as a perpetual state of conflict and alienation.

The underplaying of sensationalism in her work is undoubtedly one of the reasons her publishers have marketed all her books for "young adults," a sales device that, while it may encourage their purchase for school libraries and Christmas stockings, gives a misleading impression of their seriousness and has discouraged the quality of criticism they deserve. Although the juvenile label is made plausible by the use of children's points of view in *Nilda* and in many of the stories in *El Bronx Remembered*, the adult looking out through the children's points of view is clearly writing for people as adult as she. Only her latest book, *Felita*, was written specifically for children.

Nilda, earliest and most autobiographical of Mohr's published works, is a delightful collage of pathos, humor, nostalgia, and effective characterization. Its central image, a hidden rose garden, is a sensitive exploration of a woman's needs and their very difficult attainment. The book opens in 1941, when Nilda is ten, and closes in 1945. The community in which she lives, like Nilda herself, is young and insecure, groping its way in the corridors of a strange new world. The neighborhood is the same one where Piri Thomas grew up, and Nilda is fully aware of its lifestyle: Jimmy, her oldest brother, is an addict and pusher; Frankie, another brother, is a member of the dreaded Lightnings; Nilda discovers a knifed man clutching his bloody stomach in a hallway; she watches in horror as the hate-crazed cop brutally clubs two boys, fourteen and sixteen, members of the Pentacostal church at Lexington Avenue and 102nd Street.[2] The violence she witnesses, though rooted in a male society and to this extent accidental to Nilda's personal life, is magnified through the eyes of her innocence. But violence is never at the center of Mohr's writing and interest; her subject is the texture of everyday living, the individualization of common human experiences, especially those of childhood.

Family relations are, of course, the first and most important of these experiences, and Nilda's development grows from the influences of her mother and her stepfather, the two pivotal characters in her life. From her mother, a devout Puerto Rican Catholic, she learns how, for a woman, real existence may be lost to the unthinking demands even of children and lovers. From her stepfather she learns how personal existence can be saved in the face of any odds, even death itself. Emilio, the stepfather, is a Spanish communist, agnostic and anticlerical, and many years older than the mother. In his refusal to yield to political or religious systems, in the anger and anguish he feels when the family must apply for welfare because his chronic heart condition prevents him from working, and in his firm adherence to unpopular convictions Emilio is an unsung hero. His influence is clearly paramount in Nilda's moral and intellectual growth. His character contrasts with that of Nilda's natural father, a pleasant but morally undefined man who maintains a vaguely avuncular relationship with Nilda and her four older brothers.

The family is also used in this book to exemplify certain ethnic characteristics that Mohr would obviously like to see carried along on the journey to Americanizaton. One is the warmth and receptiveness of Nilda's family, illustrated through Sophie, whose Polish mother disowns her when Jimmy, Nilda's oldest brother, gets her pregnant. There is no question but that Sophie should move in and share Nilda's room, since Jimmy has temporarily "disappeared," a frequent happening in his world of drug dealing. After Sophie delivers a healthy black-haired son, she returns, with Nilda and the baby, to seek a reconciliation with her mother. As they enter the tenement, past the Slavic names on the mailboxes, and climb the four flights to the mother's apartment, they find themselves in a spiral of closed doors amid the dizzying smell of disinfectant. And the mother's door remains closed to Sophie's knocks and tearful entreaties; the only responses are a dog's barking and a woman's strong, accented voice saying, "My Sophie, my daughter, is dead. She died. She run off with a nigger and now she's dead."[3]

This scene, with its sense of hurt and cruelty, is a good example of Mohr's ability to isolate and bring to life the countless ego-bruising slights and humiliations that the child of poor immigrants must face: Miss Heinz at the welfare office criticizing Nilda's dirty nails; a nurse examining her head for lice and nits; a teacher, during the milk break, selling chocolate-covered cookies Nilda never has money to buy; the ubiquitous phrase "you people." The experiences radiate pain, and no pain is worse than that which children inflict on one another. At a summer camp a Spanish girl somewhat older than Nilda tells her never to claim to be Spanish because "You give us all a bad name."[4] At the same camp a group of Nilda's cottage mates deliberately cut at the fragile pride of one of their own number. Josie is a poor girl, too poor to have a suitcase, so she comes to camp carrying her clothes in a cardboard box tied with twine. She answers the laughter and derision of the other girls with pitiful fantasies about rich parents and mansions and swimming pools, which only serve to goad the others on to further cruelty. One day Josie enters the cottage and finds her cardboard box sitting on her trunk. "It was battered and had marks and words written all over it: JOSIE STINKS! JOSIE LIVES IN A GARBAGE CAN. JOSIE FOREST IS FULL OF BUGS. J.F. EATS WORMS! HA HA...HEE HEE...TAKE A BATH POOR LITTLE RICH GIRL."[5] As Josie breaks into tears and runs out of the cottage, Nilda sees some of the girls look at one another and giggle.

Pain, though vividly presented, is not one of the dominant moods of *Nilda*, which impresses more strongly with its sense of the comic, often barbed with social satire. In one very funny passage Emilio wakes from his sickbed to find the local medium driving evil spirits from the apartment with candles, herbs, a sacrificed rooster, and lots of holy water: "What is all this water on the floor? Did she pee here too? It's not enough with these fairy tales, she has to come here to pee? She can't use the toilet?"[6] Elsewhere a drunken Don Justicio crashes a Pentecostal church meeting and pees in front of the congregation to express his displeasure at his wife's presence there.

Mohr's treatment of organized religion is invariably critical or satirical. Her portrayal of the bigotry and narrowness that Nilda observes in the nuns and priest at the first summer camp she is sent to is devastating. And Nilda's dry-eyed anger at the Catholic funeral service her mother arranges for Emilio is interrupted by a suppressed giggle at the thought of her stepfather jumping out of the casket, swearing at the priest, and punching him in the nose. Nilda's religious legacy clearly came to her from "Papa."

School is another institution handled satirically, especially through teachers like Miss Maureen Reilly, the Spanish teacher whose Spanish is so poor that her Puerto Rican students can hardly understand her. Miss Reilly's class is one long crusade to correct "that dialect" her students speak at home. When her students write dirty words on the board, Miss Reilly, whose knowledge of

Spanish does not sink to that level, erases them with the comment "That's enough nonsense, girls. Always writing silly things, wasting your time. Now we must get to work. We will read and, remember, I want the correct accent on the words."[7] Other teachers, with their thinly masked contempt for the foreign and the poor and their arrogant assumption of "American" superiority and of the waywardness of people unlike themselves, show how difficult it must be for people like Nilda to emerge psychologically unharmed even from institutions designed to help them.

If Mohr criticizes some of the human components of the educational system, particularly their blindness to alternative modes of thought and feeling, she has the highest respect for education itself and the goals toward which it moves. Nilda is a good student; implicit throughout the book is the idea that only through education will she be able to become free in a society that accepts her as its own. For Nilda there is no effort toward Americanization: it is part of her growing up. During the war her brothers—except Jimmy—join the armed forces, and "Uncle" Leo gives her a war-stamp book with two dollars' worth of war stamps in it. Her interests and tastes are those of New York in the early 1940s. Nevertheless, her ties to both parents remain strong until their deaths. It is probably this continual contact with and respect for her parents' way of life that enable Nicholasa Mohr to combine, more than any other Nuyorican writer, an appreciation of Puerto Rican ethnicity with a commitment to full participation in the mores and the social structures of her native land.

What makes *Nilda* particularly satisfying, however, both within and without the context of Nuyorican writing, is its memorable comment on womanhood. The theme is initiated in the symbol of a patch of wild roses that Nilda accidentally finds hidden away in a thick cluster of bushes near her summer camp. The discovery suggests Nilda's approaching maturity, which is soon confirmed by the onset of menstruation. More than that, the garden is something private to Nilda, something that is *hers* in a very special way, since no one else knows about it. So when she brings her two closest friends to see it, she is in fact offering them a deeply personal gift—offering them, as it were, herself. The theme resurfaces later in the book when Nilda's dying mother tries to verbalize the need for just such a garden in a woman's life:

> "Do you have that feeling, honey?...That you have some-
> thing all yours...you must...like when I see you drawing
> sometimes, I know you have something all yours. Keep
> it...hold on, guard it. Never give it to nobody...not to
> your lover, not to your kids...it don't belong to them
> ...and...they have no right...no right to take it. We are
> all born alone...and we die all alone. And when I die,
> Nilda, I know I take nothing with me that is only mine."[8]

This quotation is from a long, very moving deathbed scene in which the mother, groping to reach out in love and final communication to her only daughter, is torn between maternal attachment to her children and womanly regret for the life they took from her. What Nilda knows but cannot yet express is that the inner life can be shared without being lost. The ending of the book rounds out this idea as Nilda, having developed her talent for art, shows her early drawings to her cousin and friend Claudio, pausing over the sketch of "a special trail in the woods. You see how it winds...well, that trail leads to a secret garden."[9] Nicholasa Mohr herself became a very accomplished graphic artist; her prints have appeared in major exhibitions in Puerto Rico and on the mainland.

Mohr's second book, *El Bronx Remembered,* is a collection of stories set in the South Bronx during 1945-56, a period somewhat earlier than J. L. Vivas Maldonado's stories about the same neighborhood in *A vellón las esperanzas, o Melania.* The great differences between the two books are due partly to this time difference and partly to opposite points of view. Vivas Maldonado comments perceptively about a community seen from outside. Mohr describes the world she grew up in, peopled by English speakers born for the most part in New York, mixing easily with the Jewish families still living in the neighborhood, working, going to school, unaware of themselves as part of a developing ghetto. In two of these stories the characters express their perception of themselves as a new breed, different in outlook and values from their island relatives. In "Uncle Claudio" Papi's older brother is returning in high dudgeon to Puerto Rico after only a few months in the city because he " 'doesn't get no respect here.' "[10] The most cutting hurt to Uncle Claudio's sense of dignity is in being addressed on a first-name basis by Carlito, son of a maid the family had once fired for theft back in Humacao. The occasion for Carlito's offense was a chance meeting on the subway; Carlito had no bad feelings about the old days; he even tried to give Uncle Claudio his seat and offered to fix him up with a better job than the one Papi had gotten for him. Wormwood and gall! At the end of the story Uncle Claudio's two New York-born nephews, impatient to be off to the airport and back in time for a game of stickball, still can't figure out what Carlito did wrong or what Papi means when he tries to explain that "Uncle Claudio lives in another time and that he is dreaming instead of facing life."[11] There is something more than thirteen hundred miles between Uncle Claudio's Humacao and Nicholasa Mohr's South Bronx.

In "Love with Aleluya" Joey, seconded by his friend Hannibal, makes plans to win the love of the beautiful, long-haired Serafina, a recent arrival who, Ramona cattishly notes, "can hardly speak English. She got a real thick accent. Anyway, she's such a greenhorn—."[12] Other disagreeable problems about Serafina are that she is chaperoned to and from school by a pair of taciturn older brothers and she attends services at "that alleluya church" on Friday nights instead of the dance at St. Anselm's. Nevertheless, Joey and Hannibal resolve to carry the campaign for Serafina right into enemy territory, so one evening they join the congregation at LA SALVACION DE ADAM Y EVA, *Iglesia Pentecostal del Bronx, Inc.* The services and the emergency "conversions" of the boys are described in pure slapstick, with the lovely Serafina "shrieking and waving her arms" ecstatically amid the "clapping, shouting, jumping, moving and dancing to the music [of] piano, guitar, violin and drums."[13] Stories about the conversion spread quickly, and Joey and Hannibal have to put up with some good-natured kidding before being accepted back among their own kind.

In both of these stories the point of view is of someone born and raised in New York. This sense of identity based on birthplace rather than ethnic background helps to account for the sympathy Mohr is capable of in dealing with non-Puerto Rican characters. The best example of this is "Mr. Mendelsohn," about an old Jewish man who works his way into the bosom of the Suarez family, his next-door neighbors on the South Bronx street that has been his home for forty-five years. The material could have been worked into a sentimental parable on good interethnic relations, but that point is secondary here. Mohr's emphasis is on a characterization of the old man through a study of his relationships with the individual members of the Suarez family, particularly the mother, the youngest daughter, and, later, the first grandson. The story has an interesting time structure. Mr. Mendelsohn's friendship with the family is of some years' duration, marked by the oldest son's marriage and fatherhood, but it emerges from the linear sequence of his life as an island of quiet happiness between his early struggles to raise and find husbands for his six younger sisters and his final years—after the Suarez family had bought a house around Gunhill Road—in a one-room furnished apartment his sisters found for him in a building for old people. No stone is cast here, and no special moral is established; there is only the ebb and flow of human indifference and sympathy in the great city.

Another good example of Mohr's feeling for the special qualities of living in New York is the importance she gives to pets. Two stories in this collection—one very funny, the other sad and indignant—are about affective relations between pets and people. The funny story, "A Very Special Pet," is about Joncrofo, a hen named after Mrs. Fernández's favorite movie actress. Joncrofo, a great favorite with everyone except the family cat, does wonders at keeping down the kitchen's roach population, but proves, despite the intercession of the local spiritualist healer, incapable of bearing eggs, the function for which she had been purchased. Mrs. Fernández, in an access of unnatural practicality, determines one hungry day to convert Joncrofo into a nutritious *arroz con pollo*, since the "silly hen was really no use alive to anyone."[14] The consequent battle between lady and chicken, the nick-of-time arrival of the horrified children, and Joncrofo's recovery with the help of a drop of rum are narrated with a verve and humor reminiscent of Chaucer's "Nun's Priest's Tale." The moral of the story is that the silly hen really *was* of great use, but in the impractical way that love and trust and other abstractions are of use to those who feel they cannot live by *arroz con pollo* alone.

The second pet story is about a childless couple, Don Osvaldo and Doña Nereida, owners of a small neighborhood grocery store and of a little white, fluffy-haired dog, Princess. From the attentions showered on her—expensive collars, hand-knit sweaters, a child's wardrobe unit—it is clear that Princess is the recipient of the old couple's entire store of emotional resources. She is also the only bridge across which the old couple is able to establish personal communication with other human beings.

The story is told from the point of view of Judy Morales, a young girl who loves Princess and takes her out for a walk every day after school; Princess compensates Judy for the dog her family is too poor to allow her to have. One day Don Osvaldo sells Judy's mother a can of beans which turns out to be spoiled. Rather than admit the beans are spoiled and exchange them for another can—a trivial loss to the store—he and Nereida, to prove their point, allow Judy to feed the whole can to the trusting Princess, who dies poisoned during the night. Osvaldo transmutes his cold grief into anger against the Morales family; by cutting off their credit he effectively refuses to deal with them any more, and they are forced to walk some distance to shop in another store, which offers them credit.

The scene of strongest emotional impact takes place some months later. Nereida sees Judy on the street and calls her in to ask if she would like to see where Princess used to sleep in the living quarters behind the store. Judy feels uneasy, but is unable to reject the plea of an old, lonely woman; one realizes then that the dog was a bridge not only between the storekeepers and other people, but between Nereida and Osvaldo as well. Without her each is left in a state of personal isolation which Nereida is now trying to break out of by reaching for contact with the only person she thinks might understand her love for Princess. In the back room all of the dog's things are where they had been when she died, and there hangs about the place an unpleasant odor which suggests the stench of spoiled beans, a moral correlative for the sentimental inhumanity of the old couple.

The theme of womanhood introduced in *Nilda* returns in "Her-

man and Alice," a novella. Alice, a fifteen-year-old schoolgirl, is
six months pregnant by a young man engaged to her best friend.
The social humiliation of her condition, the continual nausea,
nerves rubbed raw in the small apartment Alice shares with her
mother, stepfather, brother, and sister are the setting for the
first part of the story, which is unrelievedly bleak. Sympathy,
supportiveness, affection, even simple consideration are blatantly
wanting among members of the family, and muted hostility and
shame seem to be their dominant feelings toward others. The
reader is allowed no illusions about the kind of background
Alice comes from and the kind of people she and her parents
are. In one of her rare moments of closeness to her daughter, the
mother compares Alice's life to her own in words which suggest
a pattern that only the more fortunate of women, like Nilda,
manage to escape:

> "I had to start my life as a woman the same way, Alice—
> with you. . . . I had hoped for you it might have been differ-
> ent," her mother whispered. Alice did not answer; the
> feeling of shame choked her, and she began to cry.
>   "Ma. . . I'm sorry, Mami, I really am sorry. Really, Mami."
> Her mother held her quietly and listened as Alice tried to
> speak. After a while, her mother released her.
>   "I know, mi hijita," she said. "I know you are sorry. I
> am, too, Alice, but it's too late now. Because now, you see,
> you can be sorry for the rest of your life."[15]

But a door opens for Alice. Herman Aviles, a thirty-eight-year-
old homosexual neighbor, sensitive to Alice's unhappiness, invites her to drop into his tastefully furnished apartment occasionally as a relief from the tensions of her home life. The visits
become regular, and a sort of friendship develops and is encouraged by Alice's mother and stepfather, who find that Herman " 'is a better quality person and has wonderful manners.
He's educated, not one of those ordinarios, those loudmouths
that are coming here from Puerto Rico to El Bronx.' "[16] The friendship leads to thoughts of marriage. Alice naturally responds to
Herman's sympathy, and he genuinely wants to help her. Moreover, Herman would like to be part of a family and sees no

reason why he, Alice, and Alice's baby should not constitute one. It would be good news for his parents and brothers and sisters in Puerto Rico. Herman explains to Alice his inability to have sex with women, and she, with delivery little more than a month away, agrees that sex is not important.

They are married in St. Anselm's rectory, and Alice's baby boy is named after Herman's father. Herman remains devoted to Alice and develops a sincere affection for the child. Alice, however, grows restive under the burden of her new responsibilities in the lonely apartment; an unsophisticated teenage girl, she longs for fun—and boys. She begins to see an old girlfriend and, with Herman's permission at first, go to parties and dances, staying out later and later. Resentment soon sets in and replaces all other feelings between her and Herman. After a harsh confrontation one night, they decide to separate. Herman returns to a job in Puerto Rico with his pictures of "the baby," and Alice, as the story ends, is giving birth to a child whose father, she remembers through the pain, is her stepfather's cousin, her second man since separating from Herman.

No summary of "Herman and Alice" can do justice to the subtle moral and psychological probing that permeates the story. Self-deceit bordering on cynicism blinds all of the characters to any but the most superficial aspects of their relationships. The sex contact between Alice and the father of her first child is drab and passionless; she doesn't enjoy it, but she feels flattered at the attention. Perhaps Alice, who is young and ignorant, cannot be expected to respond differently. But Herman is equally removed from reality in finding Alice "fragile and sensitive"[17] and imagining that she might be capable of shouldering the generous but demanding proposal he makes to her. The insubstantiality of the relationship is seen in the ease with which it is dissolved.

The breakup had been painless, almost matter-of-fact. He had wished Alice lots of luck and hoped that she and Frankie would be happy. She could file for an annulment or divorce on any grounds—he would not protest. She, in turn, promised to keep him informed about Kique.[18]

On the other hand, would a relationship like that attempted by Herman and Alice be so impossible for two people less tied up in fantasies and frustrations? It would seem a better choice for Alice than repeatedly giving birth in pain and being sorry for the rest of her life.

In Nueva York, Mohr's third book, marks several departures from her earlier work. The child's viewpoint is gone, and the time setting is the present rather than a remembered past. The book is a collection of eight stories, which seem to be metamorphosing into a novel. Three characters—Rudi, Lali, and William—appear in most of the stories and interact the way characters in a long narrative do. Rudi's luncheonette, in a Lower East Side neighborhood, serves as the setting for the stories, and an orange alley cat that lives off the garbage cans in front of the buildings next door to Rudi's is a unifying leitmotif and a causative agent in the plot.

As a whole, *In Nueva York* is less successful than Mohr's earlier works, and the reasons are apparent in the first story. Beerguzzling "Old Mary," fifty-seven years old and much the worse for wear, has just received a letter from William, the illegitimate son she abandoned in Puerto Rico shortly after his birth there forty years ago. William found out about his mother's continued existence through a chance meeting with a Nuyorican couple who returned to the island; he is filled, according to his letter, with an all-encompassing desire to be united with the mother he never knew and to devote his life to her happiness. Mary has had two husbands and seven children in New York, but William becomes, in her sentimental imagination, the hope for a new life free of the dirty neighborhood, the yellow cat, the alcoholic second husband. Mary describes her sanguine expectations to her best friend, Doña Teresa, who acts like a Greek chorus in cautioning about the wages of overweening hope.

"Now, Mary, listen to me. All of this is well and good. But you don't know nothing about your son, and he is forty years old. After all, he is no youngster; he must have some ties or some past life in Puerto Rico. You should know about this."[19]

One of the basic flaws of the book is that William's past life in Puerto Rico remains a blank page throughout; it is as if forty years of life had simply blown over him, leaving no imprint on his character. He turns out to be a dwarf, and his childlike reactions when he is brought home from the airport are characteristic of what we see of him through the rest of the book: "He smiled and looked around him and then he saw her. With a swagger to his gait he rushed up the steps and embraced Old Mary, . . . 'Mama, it's you. . . it's you,' he whispered."[20] It is not clear how William recognizes his mother so unerringly, but the initial attachment persists; thereafter he always asks for her blessing before leaving the apartment to work at Rudi's or to attend night classes in English. Other than that the Mary-William relationship drops out of sight. This is terribly wasteful, because once the relationship is established, it has interesting possibilities of development, none of which is continued. Mary's initial shock at seeing William is not referred to again, and we can only speculate on what William thinks of the mother he has waited so long and come so far to be with. An author is not required to give the same amount of attention to all his characters, but in the case of Mary and William expectation and curiosity are aroused and left unsatisfied.

Another weakness is the characterization of Rudi's wife, Lali. Rudi is one year younger than Lali's father. He married her and brought her to New York from her small hometown in Puerto Rico three years after his first wife's death. Rudi's attraction toward Lali is an unstable blend of love, the habit of being married, a vague regret at being childless, and the need for someone to help out in the luncheonette; Lali is drawn by Rudi's comparative worldliness as well as by "a chance to get away—to see what was going on in other places, to live in New York, another kind of life. It just seemed exciting to me."[21] Now, two years later, the marriage has gone stale. Lali's only social contact is William, who helps her in the luncheonette and accompanies her to the English classes.

Rudi breaks a leg one day chasing the orange cat. He hires William's handsome, unstable half-brother, Federico, a would-be songwriter and experienced cook, to run the luncheonette temporarily. Lali promptly and predictably falls in love with

Federico, and they have a singularly uninteresting affair, entered into more out of kindness than passion on his part. Federico is soon frightened off by Lali's strengthening attachment, and Lali is distraught by his desertion. William "very softly and with great tenderness began to caress and make love to Lali. She responded with gratitude and compassion. In this way, together, they comforted each other."[22]

What sort of love William makes to Lali doesn't interest the reader, because the characters are uninteresting: they never reveal the sensibility or emotional depth that their roles in the book require. Mohr describes them at a distance, as if she is imagining what such characters would do under given circumstances. Perhaps the problem is in their Puerto Rican background, which is distant to Mohr, not part of her immediate experience. Sometimes she makes very improbable statements about Puerto Rico, as when Mary "left for San Juan and quickly found work in a large hotel"[23] in the middle of the depression, a time when there were few hotels of any sort in San Juan and when no one in Puerto Rico found work quickly.

The best realized character in this book is Rudi, whose middle age is fleshed out with a convincing past:

> Lali had been surprised to see Rudi as a young man, with a full head of dark hair, lean and muscular in an army uniform. He stood with his arm around a young woman and smiled happily. A large orchid corsage was pinned on her brightly flowered print dress. On the back of the photo someone had written, *Carmen and Rudi Padillo on their wedding day—April 19, 1946, Brooklyn, N.Y.*[24]

Lali's bemused reaction to the old photograph is a masterly touch, for it makes us understand things she cannot verbalize about her marriage, and it gives Rudi a temporal depth which distinguishes him from most of the other characters.

Rudi is also the most perceptive person in the book. Despite his inability to communicate with his wife on an intimate level, he has a noteworthy gift of detached observation of himself and others, and he is the first character in Nuyorican fiction to be conscious of having undergone a sea change: " 'I love Nueva

York...it's my home. I go to Puerto Rico, and I can't take the slow pace there no more. Nuyorquino...that's me now....' "[25]

Another reason for Rudi's success as a character is his sense of moral commitment, woven from the fibers of his life experience. When two teenage hoodlums rob the business he has been working so hard to build over the past sixteen years, Rudi could be a name in one of countless stories from the *Daily News*; but when, filled with harsh anger and righteousness, he runs out after them with his revolver and kills one, he steps from journalism into literature, a man requiring praise or repudiation, judgment. And when the dead boy's weak-minded mother pickets the luncheonette for two weeks to force Rudi to pay for a headstone she can't afford, his steadfast refusal, based on principle, defines him as a man of conviction and perseverence in a world of transient people and aimless emotions. At the end of the book Rudi recognizes kindred qualities in his old enemy, the orange cat that will not be deterred from raiding the garbage cans outside the store: " 'We come to terms already, eh? Anybody who lasts as long as you don't die so easy!' "[26]

As mentioned above, this book is a sort of compromise between a loosely organized novel and a collection of short stories, a genre for which Mohr has an obvious affinity and talent. Three stories from *In Nueva York*—"I Never Even Seen My Father," "The Perfect Little Flower Girl," and "The Operation"—are independent of the Rudi-Lali-William plot, though they happen to be set in the same neighborhood. The most original and interesting of these is "The Perfect Little Flower Girl," which returns to the theme of homosexuality, treating the subject with humor, though with no lack of sympathy. In this story there are two homosexual couples: Johnny and Sebastian, and Vivian and Joanna. Johnny has decided to join the army but first to marry Vivian, so that she will receive the monthly dependent's allowance and give it to the sickly Sebastian, whom Johnny supports. In contrast to these attractive but humanly marginal figures is Raquel Martínez, neighbor of Johnny and Sebastian and husbandless mother of six children whom she is managing to bring up decently with a small amount of welfare money and seasonal income from homemade *pasteles*. The mutually supportive relationship that exists between Raquel and her neighbors is evidenced in the help she gives the two men in planning the wedding and reception. Although Raquel is a good woman in every conventional sense, the hardships and precariousness of her life have made conventional prejudices meaningless to her, so she agrees to let her youngest daughter, Hilda, serve as flower girl at the wedding. At the reception Hilda entertains the guests by singing her own special arrangement of "You've Got a Friend," which is a pretty good summary of what this story is all about. Here again Mohr deepens her characterizations by searching the past: Vivian's account of her engagement to Sebastian in college, the reminiscences of Johnny's one-time foster parents, and so forth. These remembered vignettes, interesting in themselves, give this twenty-page story a resonance usually found only in much longer pieces.

Mohr's latest book, *Felita*, really *is* written for younger readers. It centers on an incident that took place in the author's life some years before the events narrated in *Nilda*:

> When I was a little girl we moved to a supposedly better neighborhood, meaning that it was less crowded, the schools were better, there was less crime—that is, to a white neighborhood. My family was constantly persecuted and brutalized and we had to move out and go back to the old neighborhood. So what happened to *Felita* happened to me many years ago when I was about six years old.[27]

Although the new neighborhood's rejection of Felita's family is the most dramatic episode in the book, it is quickly over and its most important function is to introduce the major theme: the relationship between a young girl and her paternal grandmother, who helps her to understand herself and her place in a world that is, for all its limitations, filled with hope and beauty. Related to this theme is the meaning of a neighborhood to the people who live in it, especially the children. The neighborhood that Felita's family first leaves and then returns to is what outsiders would see as a slum or ghetto. From casual comments ("Mr. Goldstein wasn't around anymore. Mr. Perez was the owner."[28]) we learn that earlier residents have already left the overcrowded streets of small *bodegas* and women shouting from windows and men in undershirts playing dominoes on stoops and sidewalks. For Felita, however, the same neighborhood is a place where she can count on love and acceptance, where most people respect a set of rules and values not visible to people looking in from the outside. The nicest of the many nice things Mohr does in *Felita* is to persuade the reader that words like *slum* and *ghetto* connote little more than a point of view.

The virtues of *Felita* are a little mirror of Nicholasa Mohr's achievement as interpreter of the Nuyorican community. Her people are more accessible than those of any other Nuyorican author with a national audience; most are decent, law-abiding, and family-oriented, and their children, most of them, will climb over the social and economic fences that contract their early years. They are not spics or other minority stereotypes: they are, in fact, curiously like people everyone knows. To have drawn such people out of a disliked and misunderstood subgroup is no small accomplishment.

Mohr's future as a writer is uncertain. It will depend to a large extent on her ability to create characters, plots, and situations beyond the personal experiences she has drawn upon up to now. She has said what she had to say about growing up Nuyorican, and she has said it well, but a continuation of this matter could only be repetitious. Despite its artistic weaknesses, *In Nueva York*, with its adult characters and contemporary setting, points the direction in which she should go. Perhaps she will turn, as few have done, to the hundreds of thousands of individuals who, like her, have left the city's Barrios and claimed full citizenship in the great metropolis.

NOTES

1. Juan Flores, "Back Down These Mean Streets," p. 53.
2. For an analysis of Mohr's changing attitudes toward Anglo authority figures see John C. Miller, "Nicholasa Mohr: Neorican Writing in Progress," *Revista/Review Interamericana* 9, no. 4 (1979/80):543-49.
3. Nicholasa Mohr, *Nilda*, p. 77.
4. Ibid., p. 135.
5. Ibid., pp. 136-37.
6. Ibid., p. 151.
7. Ibid., p. 183.

8. Ibid., pp. 234-35.
9. Ibid., p. 247.
10. Nicholasa Mohr, *El Bronx Remembered*, p. 77,
11. Ibid., p. 79.
12. Ibid., p. 138.
13. Ibid., pp. 142-43.
14. Ibid., p. 5.
15. Ibid., p. 110.
16. Ibid., p. 103.
17. Ibid., p. 115.
18. Ibid., p. 132.
19. Nicholasa Mohr, *In Nueva York*, p. 19.
20. Ibid., pp. 25-26.
21. Ibid., pp. 107-8.
22. Ibid., p. 128.
23. Ibid., p. 15.
24. Ibid., p. 105.
25. Ibid., p. 119.
26. Ibid., p. 155.
27. Edna Acosta-Belén, "Conversations with Nicholasa Mohr," *Revista Chicano-Riqueña* 8, no. 2 (1980): 40.
28. Nicholasa Mohr, *Felita*, p. 16.

6

NUYORICAN POETS

Hispanics are still very much at home with the concept of poetry as a popular art. Poetry recitals in Spain and Latin America make the same appeal as song or dance performances; the recitals are often accompanied by dance movements and music, suggesting the affinity of the three forms of expression. The poetry recited is likely to be very sentimental, and the performance may sound bombastic to ears not bred to the tradition, but they provide a cultural soil in which other types of poetry can grow. This tradition, often taking the form of impromptu recitals among family and friends, helps to account for the surprising amount of poetry composed by Puerto Ricans in New York.

The poets represent a broad range of style and subject matter. Some write in Spanish and are published in bilingual reviews like *The Rican* and *Revista Chicano-Riqueña* or in the more transitory publications of branch colleges with Puerto Rican studies programs. These writers are often well versed in the modern poetry of Puerto Rico and Latin America and see themselves as deriving from that tradition, a view supported by Alfredo Matilla and Iván Silén in their bilingual anthology *The Puerto Rican Poets/Los Poetas Puertorriqueños*. At the other end of the spectrum is Victor Hernandez Cruz, who, with four books already published and another on the way, is, despite his ethnic experience, clearly at home in contemporary American poetry and has established an increasingly solid reputation for himself with critics and serious readers.

More germane to the present study is the work of a group of young poets—mostly under forty—who, born of Puerto Rican parents, raised in New York, fluent in English and Spanish, see themselves as a hitherto unrecorded species filling a new niche in the American cultural ecology. They call themselves Nuyoricans, members of a minority group that, not having been satisfactorily accommodated in the white and monied society that is politically dominant in the United States, constitutes a subculture or parasociety with its own behavioral norms, its own esthetic, even its own dialect. That such a concept exists and serves as the basis for a poetic manifesto is brought out clearly in the introductions to two anthologies: *Nuyorican Poetry*, edited by Miguel Algarín and Miguel Piñero; and *Herejes y mitificadores: Muestra de poesía puertorriqueña en los estados unidos*, edited for Island readers by Efraín Barradas and Rafael Rodríguez with Spanish translations by Carmen Marín.

There are, of course, differences of style and sensibility among the Nuyorican poets, but their work as a whole is very homogeneous, growing as it does from shared assumptions and similar experiences. The Nuyorican Poets' Cafe at 505 East Sixth Street served as an early headquarters where Nuyoricans could meet to talk, listen to Latino music, and hear one another read poetry. The atmosphere of the readings is suggested by Algarín:

> Barbara didn't get to read because
> she was playing it like a kinder-
> garten Marm who looks over her
> spectacles at the class as she waits
> for SILENCE! meanwhile, we,
> us, you, I the tribe of ignoramuses that
> we are, we keep rapping and enjoying
> ourselves and talking and burping and
> farting till our school Marm Barbara
> fills the environment with venom
> and confusion and her pain—[1]

Poets like Allen Ginsberg, Gregory Corso, and William Burroughs visited the café and found in their Nuyorican counterparts "the kind of dynamism and vitality that they recall from the days of the Beat Generation poets in San Francisco."[2] It may be that the closed-circuit world of the Nuyorican poets will deny them the nationwide audience that the Beat Generation writers commanded; on the other hand, the inner-city minority world they inhabit is getting to look more and more like the inner soul of America's future, so their perceptions have a relevance beyond the confines of their immediate experience.

These poets see themselves as belonging to a society distinct from but operating within a dominant society that is repressive and unjust to its minorities, refusing to recognize their basic physical, moral, and spiritual needs and denying them dignity. This denial is poignantly reflected in Pedro Pietri's visions of inoffensive, frightened people struggling to make ends meet on the borderline between destitution and exploitation:

> It was the night
> before the welfare check
> and everybody sat around the table
> hungry heartbroken cold confused
> and unable to heal the wounds
> on the dead calendar of our eyes[3]

> Spic stick your tongue out
> I want to mail a letter
> Spic say goodnight
> to your employer he is
> exhausted from looking
> at you work so hard[4]

However badly one is exploited, though, work indicates membership, tangential though it may be, within the dominant society. Rejection by the society—in Bimbo's "A Job,"[5] and Pietri's "Unemployed,"[6] for example—is frequently symbolized by joblessness. It may also be symbolized by cohabitation with rats and roaches, as in Jorge Lopez's "Counterfeit Quarters," translated by Miguel Piñero:

> We have meetings with the cockroaches
> who are cockroaches in the houses of
> cockroaches who visit the vampires
> to suck the blood of the rats in 538
> east 6th st. which is my house, and drink
> beer with blood.[7]

The denial of dignity is seen as an imposed impotence in the heavy sexual imagery characteristic of Algarín:

> a man is demoralized
> when his woman and children
> beg for weekly checks,
> . . . even the fucking a man does
> on a government bought mattress
> draws the blood from his cock,
> cockless, sin espina dorsal,
> mongo—that's it!
> a welfare check is a mongo affair!
> mongo means flojo
> mongo means bloodless
> mongo means soft
> mongo cannot penetrate
> mongo can only tease
> but it can't tickle
> the juice of the earth vagina.[8]

The responses to this sense of shame are the main concern of Nuyorican poetry. One response is violence directed inward, against one's family or oneself. In "Kill, Kill, Kill" Piñero describes a man coming home to discharge his day's accumulation of frustrated anger against his wife:

> So I grabbed her by her fucking neck and threw her
> ass across the kitchen table and she went flying over
> the living room table and over the rest of the unpaid
> over priced furniture landing on the over worked bed,
> and I jumped in the air with the scream of an Apachi
> warrior's cry of battle and I kill, kill, killed. . .
> All my troubles away.[9]

The same inward-directed violence may lead to the unconsciously suicidal use of drugs, powerfully described in Pietri's "O/D":

> is your birthday again
> and you are inside the cake
> baked from the flesh
> of dead mice that fell
> from your mouth while

you bathe in the urine
after accidentally falling
into the toilet bowl
trying to spit out the nails
that your blood swallow
when your eyeballs become
the definition of wrong numbers
trying to light the ice cubes
that replaced the candles.[10]

Drugs are not always presented as suicidal: often they are seen simply as one of the many anodynes used to alleviate the shame of daily living. Pietri's people play the numbers, go to seances, watch television, buy used cars, and dream "empty dreams/ from the make-believe bedrooms/ their parents left them" as a heritage.[11] So Juan, Miguel, Milagros, Olga, and Manuel die because there is no sustenance in the "make-believe steak/ and bullet-proof rice and beans"[12] they feed on in the alien, synthetic world that surrounds without embracing them.

So what must a spic do to be saved? What positive response is there to rejection and shame? For Pietri, salvation lies in a strong affirmation of *puertorriqueñismo*, pride in one's essence and heritage:

PUERTO RICO IS A BEAUTIFUL PLACE
PUERTORRIQUENOS ARE A BEAUTIFUL RACE.[13]

This sentiment is different in a very important way from the celebration of ethnic background among other nationality groups in the United States. An Irish-American has no doubts or reserves about being an American; "Irish" merely tells something about the kind of American he is. Pietri's emphasis on Puerto Rican identity, on the other hand, connotes a resistence to americanization, the traditional goal of immigrants. Martita Morales is explicit on this point in "The Sounds of Sixth Street," about a girl who is harassed at school for refusing "to do the pledge of allegiance to the amerikan flag":

> this is a Puerto Rican girl
> trigueña and fifteen years old
> this is a Puerto Rican girl
>   to her, her flag is GOLD
> and she rebels
> and she rebels
> and for this, they want her expelled
> but she keeps on fighting
> yeah, she fights and she fights
> because she knows she is Right![14]

But the sense of being Puerto Rican is not common among Nuyorican poets, most of whom remember Puerto Rico only as a set of nostalgic images their mothers conjured up on cold winter nights. Attempts to identify with these images are apt to be disappointing. Both Piñero and Algarín returned to Puerto Rico as adults and reacted to the experience with disillusionment and anger. Some of their disillusionment—over the neon commercialization of parts of San Juan, for example, and the dominance of foreign investors in the island's economy—would strike a sympathetic chord among Puerto Rican intellectuals, who have been reacting the same way for years. But what most depressed Piñero and Algarín was not being accepted on the Island and not being able to identify with Island Puerto Ricans. Piñero speaks of "this slave blessed land/ where nuyoricans come in search of spiritual identity/ are greeted with profanity."[15] Algarín, traveling with Lucky CienFuegos, began his visit with high expectations:

>   we thought
> that getting off the plane
> would drop us into the lap
> of "la familia," we thought
> we'd find a noble feeling
> that we'd be sure and secure
> that there would be a madre
> alma to kiss our New York
> soot-filled bodies and soul.[16]

Disillusionment appears almost immediately in the person of a cop who runs Algarín in for driving with an expired license; it follows the rented VW to the little country town of Maguayo, whose chief attraction is the availability of alligator pears at fifteen cents apiece. Algarín apostrophizes the town in accents of undisguised condescension:

> Maguayo your jibaro,
> your survival
> is Nuyorican not Taino,
> not black, not white
> just Nuyorican.[17]

Piñero strikes the same note in calling to account the patriotism of Island Puerto Ricans:

> puertorriqueños cannot assemble displaying the emblem
> nuyoricans are fighting & dying for in newark, lower east side
> south bronx where the fervor of being
> puertorriqueños is not just rafael hernández.[18]

Similar reactions are recorded in poems by Amina Muñoz[19] and José Angel Figueroa.[20]

The quotations just given, with their reiterated emphasis on the term *Nuyorican*, mark the last stage in the Nuyorican poets' quest for a world they and their people can inhabit with dignity and a sense of belonging. Where *do* they belong? They have lost the land of their fathers and not yet found a way into the American mainstream. They are at home in a place where their needs for social and human recognition go unsatisfied. And so they have opted to create, within their inner-city frontiers, their own society with its own music, language, ethics, politics, and laws. It is a tricky business. Algarín, recognizing the problem raised by disparities between the codes of the outer and the inner societies, uses the term *outlaw*, with Robin Hood connotations, to refer to the Nuyorican in the context of his sociopolitical relations with mainstream society: "The outlaw is morally free to act, to aggress against authority because he realizes that that is in his power; he goes for broke whether it is for himself or for his friends or his people."[21]

Nuyoricans, however, are not outlaws in the style of the Weathermen or Fuerzas Armadas de Liberación Nacional, which seek to subvert the dominant society. Rather they see themselves as a separate but equal society with power to negotiate with the establishment. The society's executive branch may be a neighborhood gang—the Young Lords, the Renigades, the Guardian Angels—which has grown up and taken on social responsibilities in its community.[22] One example of how these gangs operate is Algarín's description of a meeting between the Dynamites and members of the local fire station:

> One of the Dynamites says: "We would like to acquire legal possession of the lot down the street. We are willing to clean it up. We could use your help." Nuyorican and English are running neck to neck. Both sides are being respected. The feelings of both parties are not in static. We are feeling balanced. The Dynamites and the firemen move into a coherence. Chief Hart looks at Captain Docherty. He snaps into recollection: "That's the lot the city offered us for a parking lot, but we never got to make use of it." The Chief looks pleased. One of the firemen consents to pitch in and work. All of the firemen finally join in consent.
>
> Two languages have met. We talked and understood each other. The outlaw meets the institution. The outlaw discovers the community needs him![23]

The renovation of abandoned buildings and the protection of neighborhood residents against burglary are other activities of these groups. The sociology of these activists is open to various interpretations. On the one hand, they can be seen as examples of good old American self-help and local initiative; on the other hand, they represent a sort of secession, part of a local third world of internally organized minorities operating with a quasi-independence within the context of the United States.[24] This concept is stressed in Algarín's travel poems: on a visit to Taos Pueblo Indian land, where he sees "brown tanned Indian red skin/ reminding me of brown Nuyorican people," there is an inescapable association of national prerogatives with minority groups:

who would the Pueblo Indian send
to a formal state meeting
with the heads of street government,
who would we plan war with?
can we transport arms earmarked for ghetto
warriors, can we construct our street
government constitutions on your land?
when orthodox Jews from Crown Heights
receive arms from Israel in their territorial struggle
with local Brooklyn Blacks,
can we raise your flag
in the Lower East Side
as a sign of our mutual treaty of protection?[25]

The mention of Brooklyn blacks serves as a reminder of black
emigratory and secessionist activity as far back as Marcus Gar-
vey. It also serves as a reminder that Algarín's politicized vocabulary is not simply metaphor.

Attachment to a specific neighborhood is strong in Nuyorican
poetry, and the neighborhood is precisely defined by its boundaries. "From Houston to 14th Street/ from Second Avenue to the
mighty D" is where Piñero wants his ashes scattered:

I don't wanna be buried in Puerto Rico
I don't wanna rest in long island cemetery
I wanna be near the stabbing shooting
gambling fighting & unnatural dying
& new birth crying
so please when I die...
don't take me far away
keep me near by
take my ashes and scatter them thru out
the Lower East Side...[26]

Sometimes the sense of geographic definition narrows down to
a single building. Algarín's apostrophe to Maguayo ends in self-
definition concretized in an address:

te amo por la simplicidad
que le ofreces
a uno who lives in
524 E. 6th St.
New York, New York
10009. [27]

This shift from Spanish to English as the poet prepares to turn home again illustrates the importance of language in Nuyorican thought and poetics, the importance lying in the significance of language in cultural and personal identity. The Nuyorican's marginal position in American society often leads him to strained, ambiguous attitudes toward the use of English, the language of the oppressor—and more often than not the Nuyorican's own first language. Pietri, for example, praises the intelligence of his grandmother, who has been in New York for twenty-five years "and does not speak/ a word of English."[28] Algarín asks for boiling water and lye "to soothe my soiled lips/ for the english that i/ speak betrays my need to be/ a self made power."[29] But speaking Spanish would not make Algarín a "self made power" either: that would be even further from the truth of the Nuyorican experience. What most second-generation Nuyoricans speak is two languages: Spanish with Spanish-speakers, English with English-speakers, and among themselves a protean mix of the two in any and all combinations, which goes by the name of Spanglish or Nuyorican. Some speak broken English or *español matao*, and some a variety of black English. All of these options, individually or in combinations, are exploited by the Nuyorican poets to different degrees. Tato Laviera uses more Spanish than the other poets mentioned here and humorously interprets his bilingualism as the ability to speak neither of two languages:

how are you?
¿como estás?
i don't know if I'm coming
or si me fui ya

si me dicen barranquitas, yo reply,
"con qué se come eso?"
si me dicen caviar, i digo,
"a new pair of converse sneakers."[30]

Pietri plays with subtler characteristics of Nuyorican speech;
"We do not want to be/ destroy diminish and finish forever
america"[31] not only mimics the Spanish speaker's tendency to
simplify final consonant clusters in English, but also creates a
line that would not work out at all if the dental endings of the
past participles were present. In "Je me souviens" Algarín remembers Canada in three languages:

> Trudeau parle a son Canada
> through'video lines,
> invoking l'unification d'esprit du Canada,
> San Juan Bautista est aussi
> el patrón en la isla en que nací[32]

But for vitality and joy in language play it would be hard to
match Piñero, whose amalgam of English, Spanish, jive talk,
and street rhetoric dances through the opening lines of "Jitterbug Jesus," a title which is itself full of energy:

> Tiempos is longin' lookin'
> for third world laughter
> to break out like a pimple on the face
> of a pimp
> of youthful
> latino eyes that chase el ritmo del guiro
> en los vagones del tren on school mornin'
> shoutin' broken spanish dream
> —si tú cocina como tu mamá
> como hasta el pegao
> jitterbuggin' in wrinkled
> worn out jeans
> bailando new found pride in bein' nuyoricano....[33]

Anyone who can use language that well has earned his pride.

Another important element in Nuyorican culture is music,
with overtones of race and class. There are lots of poems written
about music and musicians: Algarín's "Ray Barretto: December
4, 1976," "A Salsa Ballet: *Angelitos Negros*," and "Sylvester's 'Step
II' "; Laviera's "canción para un parrandero," "the africa in pedro
morejón," "tumbao (for eddie conde)," "the salsa of bethseda
fountain," and others. Almost invariably the music is African-

inspired and rooted in Latin America. For Laviera music expresses the fundamental African component throughout the Caribbean—and the Caribbean New York:

> I hear the merengue in french haiti
> and in dominican blood,
> and the guaracha in yoruba,
> and the mambo sounds inside the plena
> so close to what i really understand,
> sometimes i think'
> that cuba is africa,
> or that i am in cuba and africa at the
> same time, sometimes i think africa
> is all of us in music.[34]

Music also expresses the essential identity of Hispanic and American blacks in "the salsa of bethseda fountain," where popular Puerto Rican music is seen as "meaning the same as marvin gaye/ singing spiritual social songs/ to black awareness."[35] Laviera's Spanish poetry, in particular, is influenced by Caribbean negritude poetry, one of whose best known practitioners was the white Puerto Rican Luis Palés Matos, whom Laviera refers to in "canción para un parrandero." On the other hand, Jesús Papoleto Meléndez's "rare culture" of Puerto Rican and southern black cuisines in "OYE MUNDO/ sometimes" is an autochthonous growth from the soil of a common ghetto experience.[36]

Like other themes in Nuyorican writing, black self-awareness is imposed by sociopolitical conditions; the racist values of the majority promote among the darker-skinned Hispanics a sense of identification with the anglophone blacks, whose place in the social structure is established. This shift to race as a dominant factor in self-assessment breaks with the norms still prevalent in Puerto Rico, where people define themselves more in terms of language, class, and nationality than of race. Nuyorican identification with blacks of different linguistic and cultural background suggests an increasing differentiation between insular and migrated Puerto Ricans.

If sociopolitical observations weigh heavily in this account of Nuyorican poetry, it is because much of the poetry derives from sociopolitical experience and because the poets regard themselves as community poets, the community serving as both inspiration and audience. Nevertheless, a poet *is* a poet precisely because he has talents not shared by other members of the community he represents. His use of these talents—sensitivity to experience, originality, intelligence, feel for language, for example—defines his aesthetic achievement and makes it possible to evaluate him by comparison with poets of other times and places. So although this chapter has concentrated on what Nuyorican poets have to say about their Nuyorican world, something must be said about the less parochial aspects of their work from the viewpoint of a disinterested reader.

The first thing to say about Nuyorican poetry as a whole is that it is a young poetry written over the past ten years or so by poets who see themselves as the first chroniclers of a new pattern of communal life. They write, therefore, more about their experiences than about themselves, and since they have been exposed to the same experiences, their subject matter is repetitive. Except for their sometimes vivid descriptions of drug states, they are not introspective. They have little sense of intellectual discipline, so their social comments often take the form of rhetorical preaching rather than perceptive criticism. Algarín, as the leading theoretician for the group, is especially vulnerable to this temptation, and it weakens the value of his ideas; great public poets, Wordsworth and Yeats among them, have been those whose rhetoric is picked clean by a critical intellect. The need for critical intellect also shows itself in the wildly uneven quality of the work published. *Nuyorican Poetry* includes poems ranging from brilliant to remarkably bad. To develop a real capacity for self-criticism, the Nuyorican poets could use more criticism from outside, preferably from other poets, poets different from themselves.

With all these limitations, Nuyorican poetry has the inestimable virtue of being fun to read. And the reader need no more be a Nuyorican than a reader of Homer need be a Greek. People who have turned away from the hermetic poetry of the past half century will find that many Nuyorican poems are surprisingly good and at the same time accessible. Despite the depressing circumstances that clothe them, many are inwardly optimistic, asserting faith in the possibilities of life beyond the accidents of poverty, drugs, and discrimination. This faith is expressed most movingly in their language, a joyous, creative, and at times quite sophisticated blend of different registers of Spanish and English.

Multilingual poetry is nothing new in literature. Its most familiar manifestation in the Western European literary tradition is medieval macaronic verse, combining Latin and one or more vernaculars. There is no question of any influence here: it is completely improbable that the Nuyorican poets are familiar with any multilingual verse other than their own, which derives from everyday usage rather than literary tradition. What is interesting is the similarity of use and technique between medieval and Nuyorican verse in the hands of poets so dissimilar in literary education—a good example of completely independent origins for traditions that are very much alike. The use of Spanish and English in Nuyorican verse, while it expands the poet's resources, limits his audience. This limitation is unimportant as long as the poets are satisfied to write for one another and for their own community. It will become more problematical when they begin to address themselves to a more heterogeneous public, as some are already doing.

Victor Hernandez Cruz, who has published more and received far more critical recognition than any of the other poets mentioned here, writes in English. He does not, despite common experiences, share the ideological and esthetic commitments of poets who are self-consciously Nuyorican, and he is not represented in the Algarín-Piñero anthology, the best indicator of who belongs and who doesn't. His meticulously poised language, speaking to the eye more than the ear, is evident in the following description of a drug experience:

> the walls
> colorful paints
> things
> big-breasted monkeys
> white priests
> with pumpkin-faces
> talking books
> a pissing t.v. set
> strangers walking naked

flying in the air
a kissing horse
a boat coming from that building.[37]

This pictorial brilliance of Hernandez Cruz sometimes leads to almost pure verbal abstraction, poles apart from the Nuyorican poetry of feeling and statement.

Pietri has attracted a wider readership than most of his poetic colleagues, partly because he seldom mixes languages perhaps, but mostly because he has a talent adequate to express a highly individual perceptiveness in persuasive metaphor. His language is alive with sudden juxtapositionings that manage to make their point without disrupting the poem:

in ponce
there is a beach
without broken glass
in the sand
the ocean has
twenty-twenty vision
is safe to breathe
on this beach
there are no splinters
in the wind.[38]

Included in his *Puerto Rican Obituary* is "Suicide Note from a Cockroach in a Low Income Housing Project." The narrator of this long and very funny poem is a protean cockroach, sometimes male and sometimes female, speaking on behalf of its "people" to protest the discrimination they are subjected to at the hands (and feet) of minority groups living in "these damn housing projects." Pietri's inventiveness in playing with basic American clichés, including clichés about serious matters like racism and poverty, raises the poem at times to great mock-epic exhuberance:

We are the real american
We was here before columbus
We was here before general electric
We was here before the ed Sullivan show
We are older than adam and eve
Noah also took cockroaches into his ark
Why should we be denied coexistènce???[39]

Despite the favorable reactions *Obituary* prompted in critics and readers, Pietri has not published any succeeding volume. It is hard to see why. His more recent poems, especially "Underground Poetry" and "Love Story," are characterized by the same exhuberance of imagination combined with greater discipline of structure and language.

Most of the critical recognition awarded Piñero up to now has been for his plays. He is well represented in *Nuyorican Poetry* but has published only one slender volume of his own. However, this limited poetic output is enough to signal a major talent. In poems like "The Book of Genesis According to San Miguelito" and "Visitin' a Friend at the Cold Shop," from *La Bodega Sold Dreams*, he captures Pietri's irreverent irony. His most characteristic poems, however, are autobiographical and lyrical, filled with a Runyonesque affection for a city which, dirty and cold as it can be, is an exciting stage for the enactment of the poet's only life. Piñero works with the same materials as the other Nuyorican poets—the rat- and roach-tunneled tenements, the crime- and drug-ridden streets—but from them he manages to create, at his best, poems touched with love and dignity and joy. He has been able to see beyond the surface connotations of his world to a personal vision that is the stuff real poetry is made of. His work, curiously, often contains unexpected similarities to earlier poetry, which, in view of his scant formal education, he has probably never read. An interesting example of this similarity is the remarkable harvest poem "Twice a Month is Mother's Day," in which Piñero remembers being a little boy waiting with his mother and all the other mothers on the Lower East Side street for the mailman to bring the welfare checks, their bimonthly "harvest." The poem is filled with a sense of public festivity through which the structure and mores of the community are explored and commented on, as when the poem's Corinna presents her case before the chorus of neighborhood gossips:

> AHAHAHAHaaa here comes doña rosa she is pretty—NO she is
> beauuttiiiffuullll
> NO she is prettier than "pretty please with sugar on top" . . . wow
> she says the investigator came around last night & almost caught
> don miguel—who is the nené's tío—everyone says sí-sí-sí-sí Y que
> mas—

didn't find don miguel—pero—he found his shoes—everyone says
  sí-sí-sí
Y que mas she says they belong to her son rikie—he says tooooo
  biiiggg
everyone says sí-sí-sí-sí Y que mas—she says now he wants to
  sleep with
her or he'll never give back her checke & this time for good—everyone
  says sí-sí-sí-sí Y que mas—she says que se va hacer
when me & Mama are leavin' i ask doña rosa why the investigator
  wants
to sleep with her—coño I don't even like sleepin' with my two
  hermanos—everyone was feelin' good cus they all start laughin'.[40]

Piñero's plays, discussed in the next chapter, deepen this feeling for community mores into a persistent concern over the
social boundaries of morality.

NOTES

1. Miguel Algarín, *Mongo Affair*, p. 52.
2. David Vidal, " 'Nuyorican' Poetry Flowers in New York Cafe,"
San Juan Star, Portfolio Section, 18 May 1976, p. 1.
3. Pedro Pietri, *Puerto Rican Obituary*, p. 12.
4. Ibid., p. 23.
5. Miguel Algarín and Miguel Piñero, eds., *Nuyorican Poetry*, p. 93.
6. *Obituary*, p. 98.
7. *Nuyorican Poetry*, p. 44.
8. *Mongo*, pp. 87-88.
9. Miguel Piñero, *La Bodega Sold Dreams*, p. 20.
10. *Obituary*, p. 44.
11. Ibid., p. 4.
12. Ibid., p. 2.
13. Ibid., p. 10.
14. *Nuyorican Poetry*, p. 51
15. *La Bodega*, p. 14.
16. *Nuyorican Poetry*, p. 139.
17. Ibid., p. 145.
18. *La Bodega*, p. 14.
19. *Nuyorican Poetry*, p. 109.
20. Efraín Barradas and Rafael Rodríguez, eds., *Herejes y mitificadores*,
p. 80.
21. *Nuyorican Poetry*, p. 27.

22. For insight into the evolving and increasingly self-conscious neighborhood "gang" see the handsomely photographed and printed *Palante: Young Lords Party*, by Michael Abramson and others.

23. *Nuyorican Poetry*, pp. 17-18.

24. The local third world metaphor seems to be fairly widespread among minority groups. See Joseph Bruchac, ed., *The Next World: Poems of Third World Americans* (Trumansberg, N.Y.: The Crossing Press, 1978).

25. Miguel Algarín, *On Call*, p. 58.

26. *La Bodega*, p. 8.

27. *Nuyorican Poetry*, p. 145.

28. *Obituary*, p. 105.

29. *Nuyorican Poetry*, p. 58.

30. Tato Laviera, *La Carreta Made a U-Turn*, p. 7.

31. *Obituary*, p. 25.

32. *On Call*, p. 53.

33. *La Bodega*, p. 17.

34. *U-Turn*, p. 43.

35. Ibid., p. 53.

36. Jesús Papoleto Meléndez, *Street Poetry & Other Poems*, p. 2.

37. Vicor Hernandez Crus, *Snaps*, p. 103.

38. *Obituary*, p. 104.

39. Ibid., p. 26.

40. *Nuyorican Poetry*, p. 124.

7
MOVING OUT

Most of the literature discussed up to now has been a response to the challenge of growing up as part of New York's Puerto Rican community—mostly Spanish Harlem, the South Bronx, and the Lower East Side—where a new and evolving pattern of life demanded self-study and evaluation. That self-study is still going on and will continue as the community changes and as new people react to it with fresh insights. At the same time, some Nuyorican writers have begun to look outside El Barrio and deal with other interests, either personal concerns or broader social contexts. While it is still too early to attempt a full and systematic coverage of these interests, signs of new directions can be pointed out which mark either new social developments or a broadening of individual horizons.

The plays of Miguel Piñero show a melting of the contours of the Nuyorican community and the substitution of other social groupings of which Nuyoricans form a part. American blacks are usually a conspicuous component of these groupings, American whites less so. Even though ethnic differences are recognized and sometimes used as identity symbols, they do not function as determiners of intragroup enmities or alliances. Piñero's stage Nuyoricans are English-speakers, seldom using Spanish even among themselves, except for occasional word borrowings. His plays present and argue out abstract moral issues against the background of crude surface realism. These characteristics can be seen in his two published plays of the nine that have been produced.

His first play, *Short Eyes*, won the New York Drama Critics Circle Award as the best American play for 1973-1974 and was produced by Joseph Papp at Lincoln Center. It is outstanding among American prison literature, partly for its emphasis on the human condition rather than on prison conditions and partly for its vision of a prison as a homogeneous society in which officials, guards, and inmates act, through their different roles, from similar motives toward similar ends. The central figure of *Short Eyes* is Juan, described as a Puerto Rican in his early thirties and referred to by such terms as poet and guru by his fellow prisoners. Juan is, most importantly, a man of understanding, a man able to enter into real human relationships because he is not controlled by the passions that limit the freedom of others: Paco's homosexual lust, El Raheem's fanaticism, prison guard Nett's furious hatred of child molesters.

Nett's passion touches off the main action of the play. A new prisoner, Clark Davis, is added to the floor, and Nett maliciously lets the others know he has been accused of child molesting, the basest of offences in the code of ethics recognized by prison society:

> Sit down, Murphy...I'm talking to this...this scumbag ...yeah, he's a child rapist...a baby rapist, how old was she? How old?...Eight...seven...Disgusting bastard....I hope to God that they take you off this floor, or send you to Sing Sing...The men up there know what to do with degenerates like you.[1]

Incited by Nett's words, the others taunt and abuse Clark in a grotesque parody of children bullying a scapegoat. They derive a sense of righteousness from his condemnation. The most violent of his tormentors is "Shoe" Murphy, the only other Anglo prisoner on the floor. Shoe's aggressiveness toward Clark is a sort of inverse expression of the lingering racism seen when Nett breaks up a fight Shoe is losing to El Raheem.

The only person in the prison who listens to Clark—and to whom Clark is able to talk honestly about himself—is Juan. In a long, moving conversation, which takes place when they are left alone in the dayroom, Clark shows himself a sad, seriously disturbed human being who is, in fact, a chronic abuser of little girls but who has no memory of the particular act he is accused of, though he cannot deny it might have happened. The confession becomes the laying down of a terrible burden, and Clark gives Juan the epithets "the listener. . . the compassionate."[2] Juan realizes too late that listening confers responsibility:

JUAN
Why the hell did you have to make me your father confessor? Why? Why didn't you stop, why?

CLARK
Cause you asked. Cause you. . .What I told you I didn't even tell the doctors at the observation ward. . .Everything is coming down on me so fast. . .I needed to tell it all. . .to someone. . .Juan, you were willing to listen.[3]

Juan's sense of responsibility proves ineffectual in the course of events already set in motion. The climax begins when all the prisoners except Juan determine to sodomize Clark. Nett sees what is happening and doesn't interfere. Clark, showing more spirit than before, threatens to report them, including Nett. This threat is what brings them, with Nett's approval, to kill him and claim it was suicide. With Juan held powerless by the others, Shoe slashes Clark's throat. The murder is rationalized as an execution for Clark's contemptible offense; actually it is the breakdown of the fragile humanity they had managed to preserve in the contaminated prison society. The ensuing moral anarchy receives official sanction when Allard, the investigating officer, destroys evidence that would have given the lie to the suicide story and revealed Nett's complicity:

NETT
Thank you, sir.

ALLARD
There's nothing to thank me for. I didn't do this for you, Nett, but for the Department. Do we understand each other?

NETT
Yes, sir.[4]

While Nett and Allard justify their guilt on the basis of institutional good, the moral issues are forced on the prisoners' consciences when they learn that Clark had been proven innocent of the charge against him. Juan does not tell them of Clark's confession of other acts of child molesting: that would merely allow them to justify themselves with an excuse that has, in fact, no relevance to the moral issue. Their reactions to the news vary. Shoe refuses to accept Clark's innocence: "Man, he was guilty, I know, I could tell, I could see it in his eyes."[5] Paco, the most passionate in the move to sodomize Clark, is morally bankrupt, hence unaffected: "What difference does it make? I took part? I saw him guilty. I feel nothing, mistake, it happens, eso pasa."[6] As the play ends, the possibility of personal redemption exists only for those who, like Ice, are willing to accept their burden of guilt:

ICE
Cupcakes, listen to me, you killed him just as much as I did.

CUPCAKES
You? You wasn't even there.

ICE
I was there . . . I was there . . . No, I didn't swing the knife . . . and neither did you, but we're guilty by not stopping it . . . We sanctioned it . . . Only Juan is free . . .[7]

It is exciting to watch this sensitive morality play take shape from the indecencies and brutalities of prison life and to realize that Piñero wrote it while a prisoner at Sing Sing, a circumstance that illuminates his characteristic questioning and restructuring of conventional attitudes and value systems.

The most successful of Piñero's later plays, *The Sun Always Shines for the Cool*, under an exhilarating surface of rhythmic vitality, is an allegory on the source and nature of morality. The setting is a bar run by a man named Justice and patronized mostly by pimps and their "stables." Most of the patrons are black or remotely Puerto Rican, but the ethnic distinctions have no importance. Since nicknames are used instead of real ones, the text gives little information about ethnic background, and ethnicity plays no role in establishing relationships. What differentiates the characters from one another is their understanding of and adhesion to a set of rules that constitutes a moral center from which their lives are played out.

The play introduces its theme in the first few lines: Phebe, one of the whores, is sternly reprimanded for turning her back to the bar, a serious offense. As a punishment Justice "runs the bar" on Phebe's pimp, Cat Eyes; running the bar on someone means making him pay for all the drinks ordered during a fixed period of time. Cat Eyes, as Phebe's pimp, is expected to assume responsibility for her actions. His unwillingness to do so and his failure to follow the rules of the game bring swift criticism from Justice:

> CAT EYES: Running the bar on me? Justice, you must be clear out of your mind...I ain't paying for nobody's drinks...
>
> JUSTICE: Cat Eyes, there are many unwritten rules in the game that you play...this is a hustler's place...all my customers are players, and they go with the rules...the same ones that are out in the street apply here. One...the major, is respect...you don't disrespect the place...if you turn your back on the bar you disrespect me...and if you disrespect me...you pay.
>
> CAT EYES: I have never placed my back on the bar.
>
> JUSTICE: She did...she's yours...you're responsible.[8]

The responsibility Justice refers to is derived from a master-slave relationship which no one in the play questions; in fact, pimps "sell" girls to one another, and the girls seem to have no meaning apart from the pimps, to whom their relationship is, from an outsider's point of view, abject humiliation and self-abasement. The girls themselves see nothing wrong with their position, which they discuss with no hint of shame or regret. Rosa is proud of being Junior Balloon's favorite, "cuz with me it's real feeling that pour out of him in bed. I am the one who gets it hard for him before he fucks any of the other girls, cuz I know what makes him make it move. I know him...and I am the youngest of the stable."[9]

Rosa and Junior share a lifestyle that is sanctioned by the code. But Cat Eyes, who turns out to be Rosa's brother, is condemned because he was her lover and pimp before selling her to Junior.

Willie Bodega says, "Man, he started out on his own family, man, that's out," and Diamond concludes, "He needs to die."[10] Why? Even if the prohibition against incest is strong in most societies, there is no absolute necessity for its application in Justice's world. On the other hand, there is no reason why incest should not be condemned there either. It is neither more nor less transcendental than turning one's back on the bar.

Rules also change from one situation to another, as from one game to another, and sometimes they have to be made up as one goes along: "Every player is a poet. . .an actor. . .statesman. . .a priest. . .but most of all he's a player, making up rules as he passes the next car on this highway."[11] Frequent use of the words *player* and *game* in this drama is significant. A player is a pimp, but he is also one who plays games, which are limited sets of rules with no serious connection to contexts outside themselves; if one tries to apply game rules to wider social contexts, the law may be broken, and this conflict of rules underlies Algarín's discussion of Piñero as outlaw: "For many reasons Piñero came out fighting. He has fought for his use of words. He has fought for his drugs, and he has fought when he's gotten caught ripping off a pad so that he can keep his chemical cool."[12] Games are specifically linked to the outlaw concept when Willie Bodega tells of his brother's last shoot-out with the police; the brother becomes a sort of Byronic hero, and Willie identifies him with Satan:

> I'm sorry he dead, dig, but I'm proud at the way he went, man, real proud at the way he went. . . .He was a rebel. He was Satan in heaven fighting God for a piece of the action man. That's who he was, Lucifier, fighting God for a piece of the action.[13]

The game morality that runs through the piece is, however, challenged by the moral presuppositions of the main plot. As the play opens, Viejo, an old friend of Justice's, has just finished an eighteen-month sentence for drug pushing and has returned to see his daughter Chile, whom he had abandoned as a young girl to the care of Justice. Chile is now helping Justice run the bar at night and going to college during the day to become a social worker. She hates Viejo, "that man that fucked my mother and created a child who he named Chile Girl Rivera."[14] Viejo has repented of having abandoned her and ruined her mother and has returned to see what can be done about piecing together the broken shards of his past. Like Justice, he is a sort of prophet and interpreter of the code.

Chile is in love with the glib Cat Eyes, who has her convinced that he loves her and will share a good life with her once he retires from pimping and opens a bar of his own, "something that brings you respect as well as a decent living."[15] Cat Eyes really intends, once he has gained emotional control over the beautiful Chile, to turn her out—make her part of his stable. Viejo discovers this, and the main action of the play consists in his unmasking Cat Eyes to Chile and saving her from a life of prostitution. This recognition of conventional morality raises serious problems in relation to Piñero's philosophy and his attitude towards his characters. If pimps and whores are players in a game that is to be judged by its own rules—the position maintained throughout most of the play—the use of conventional ethics as the mainspring of the plot brings in a note of make-believe touching all the other assumptions. If it would be degrading or even just disappointing for a nice girl like Chile to join a stable, what about all those other pretty girls strutting their enslaved sex over the stage so unreflectively? Aren't they to be taken seriously? Or is it Chile who isn't to be taken seriously?

These are questions rather than judgments, for different interpretations are possible. Perhaps Chile's danger lies not in loving a pimp, but in loving the wrong pimp, one who doesn't understand the code. Perhaps Piñero is passing judgment on game morality by drawing on the reader's response to traditional attitudes. The existence of these and other possibilities is a measure of the complexity and interest of *The Sun Always Shines for the Cool*. And the moral complexity, far from slowing down the action, contributes to the work's immense vitality. Filled with laughter, vulgarity, flashiness, music, and lots of good guys and dolls, this play is, like Piñero's best poetry, a rejoicing in human life in any and all of its manifestations.

The setting of Piñero's plays, a world increasingly independent of outside patterns and ethnic loyalties, is one of the ways

Nuyorican writing has been going. A very different direction has been taken by Jaime Carrero, most amphibian of authors who deal with Puerto Rico's New York scene. Carrero was born and raised on the Island, then spent four year studying art in New York, in addition to later graduate study at Pratt Institute. The mainland experience has had a permanent influence on his work. Indeed, he was the first to call attention to the term *Neorican* in his 1964 *Jet Neorriqueño: Neo-Rican Jetliner*, a volume of poems in Spanish and English. He was also among the first to experiment with Spanish-English macaronic verse and has contributed to bilingual journals like *The Rican, Revista Chicano-Riqueña,* and *Revista/Review Interamericana*. His plays have been produced by Island companies and by New York's Puerto Rican Traveling Theater, which, like Carrero, has also managed a foothold in two cultures and two languages. Most of Carrero's novels and plays are written in Spanish. What distinguishes him from the writers discussed in Chapter 2 is the persistence of his interest in the *colonia* and his sympathy with the Nuyorican viewpoint, which make him one of the foremost interpreters of the Nuyorican experience for insular Puerto Ricans like himself.

The best known of Carrero's Barrio plays is *Pipo Subway no sabe reir*, a small classic among books written about children. The Nuyorican milieu is entirely convincing, but the real achievement of the play is the portrayal of Pipo, a twelve-year-old boy whose desire for a bicycle is frustrated by his mother's still-another pregnancy. The excellent dialogue and the economy of action, coupled with fine characterizations, take this play well beyond the limits of simply ethnic literature.

Another of Carrero's plays produced by the Puerto Rican Traveling Theatre is *The FM Safe*, and existentialist study of a middle-age couple who run a liquor store in a neighborhood where criminality and violence have so taken hold that individuals can survive only through personal resourcefulness and courage. A Nuyorican ghetto lends itself well to this theme, but the play suffers from excessive wordiness, irrelevancies in the action and dialogue, obvious symbolism, and an unconvincing resolution. It stands in disappointing contrast to the formal excellence of *Pipo*, and the experience described sounds imagined rather than known directly. Carrero's latest drama, *El Lucky Seven*, was produced at the University of Puerto Rico in 1979 but has not yet been published. It is a quiet, well-written play about Nuyorican adaptation to New York in the transition from first to second generation. The young boy the plot centers on repeats Carrero's success with juvenile characters in *Pipo*.

The most interesting of Carrero's novels, *Raquelo tiene un mensaje*, is one of the few books that study the cultural readjustments faced by Nuyoricans who return to the Island after having been born or spent most of their lives in New York. It is the story of Wayne Rodríguez, who had been taken north when he was five and is now returning with an MA from Columbia University to teach grammar school English in a town identified as Pueblo S in southwestern Puerto Rico. Like some of the books written by Puerto Rican writers about New York, *Raquelo* is critical and subtly satiric. The main object of the satire is what Wayne calls "la camisa de fuerza de la educación en Puerto Rico" [*the straight-jacket of education in Puerto Rico*][16]—the inflexibility of the school system, the narrowness of its administrators, the equation of good teaching with stultifying adherence to lesson plans. As a visitor from abroad (most people type him as an *americano* and call him "Mr. Wayne") Carrero's protagonist has a sharp eye for the characteristics of the "sociedad estancada" [*stagnant society*][17] he finds in Pueblo S, a town which he takes as representative. He is irritated by the slowness and inefficiency of workers, the institutionalized gossip, rewards granted for connections and favors rather than for achievement, the habit of playing things safe, the paucity of idealism.

Wayne's irritations undoubtedly reflect Carrero's, but author and character are not identical. Carrero would never have experienced Wayne's trouble with the correct use of Spanish second-person pronouns, nor would he have run into the impasses in communication that sometimes beset Wayne, making him feel like an intruder in his native land. But these are precisely the sorts of problems that return migrants encounter. Carrero's successful and sympathetic presentation of a return migrant's point of view shows how deeply he was affected by mainland habits and attitudes.

Another and in some ways better novel about a return migrant is Pedro Juan Soto's *Ardiente suelo, fría estación*, published in translation as *Hot Land, Cold Season*. The protagonist is Eduardo, who decides to celebrate his high school graduation in New York by visiting his brother Jacinto in Puerto Rico, which they had left ten years earlier and to which Jacinto had returned after his marriage, partly because he felt he belonged there and partly to get far away from his alcoholic father and long-suffering mother. The father and mother are constantly present through conversations and letters, and it is the well-developed texture of family relationships that gives depth to this novel, whose theme is the disorientation and cultural uprooting of Puerto Ricans who grow up in *la urbe*.

Like Carrero, Soto looks upon the local scene through the eyes of his protagonist, and some of his perceptions are very fine, particularly the sense of the middle-class housing development where Jacinto and his wife Adela live, and Caramillo, the hometown warped in memory. But Soto's real subject is neither Puerto Rico nor New York, but the no-man's-land between them that is inhabited by Puerto Ricans who grew up in the City. These are referred to as stammerers and people without a country, unable to relate to either of their two noncultures. Eduardo, striving honestly to understand himself at a critical stage of his life, becomes the representative of this group. Jacinto, who shares many of his brother's uncertainties and recognizes the Island's limitations, has achieved a measure of stability through his determination to remain in Puerto Rico and adapt himself to the only cultural and spiritual heritage accessible to him. In this he is unique among the "New Yorkers" who people the book. Most of these are people with fairly good education and good jobs. Cut off from family ties and local associations, they seek one another out in San Juan bars to share casual sex and tipsy nostalgia for the Big Town that was never really theirs. The "right sort" among them, including many homosexuals, constitute a club, a sort of ersatz society of their own. At the climax of the book Eduardo attends his first meeting of the club, which, in parody of a sacred rite, turns into a messy bisexual orgy.

Soto's thesis is interesting, but his obvious moral commitment, his tone of cultural righteousness, and the hopeless vacuum his characters inhabit detract from the confiability of his novel. One looks in vain here for some recognition of the tens of thousands of return migrants who, with money and skills and linguistic ability brought back from the mainland, have bought houses and started little businesses and go to church and raise decent families in Carolina and Bayamón and Toa Baja's Levittown. The successful, confident return migrants are represented more favorably by Barry Levine's *Benjy López: A Picaresque Tale of Emigration and Return*, a transcription of a return migrant's oral account of his youth in Puerto Rico, years with the army in Panama and Germany, return to civilian life and New York, and finally resettlement on the Island. "Benjy" is not an attractive figure: he is insensitive, vulgar, aggressive. But he is successful because he has learned to multiply his experiences advantageously in the ongoing competition between him and the part of the world that happens to be around him. What Levine seems to be pointing out in this essentially sociological exercise is that the migratory experience—in this case a Puerto Rican's exposure to new places and new challenges—sharpens the migrant's ability to deal with life situations successfully.

Another book dealing with the experiences of a returned migrant is *Hello Stranger*, Ester Comas's reminiscences about her life in Puerto Rico after returning there from a successful singing career in New York. Like "Benjy," Miss Comas shows a great deal of initiative; in fact, her main reason for returning is "to take part in this campaign—Operation Bootstraps—which Gov. Muñoz Marín was promoting in Washington."[18] But her efforts in the restaurant business and in the encouragement of local arts and industries run into numerous petty setbacks and frustrations, partly from the incompetence of people she has to deal with and partly from the resentment her go-to-itiveness arouses in a male-dominated society. *Hello Stranger* is persuasive and entertaining, but the events it narrates and the perception of those events are so tied up with the author's personality that it would be ingenuous to interpret them as typical.

Books about reverse migration do more than recount the return of Puerto Rican migrants to their homeland: they are also a route through which the Nuyorican experience is brought into the mainstream of Puerto Rican Literature. The opposite direction in which Nuyorican writing can go—and eventually lose itself—is toward merger with mainstream literature in the United States. A good example of this direction is the work of Edwin Torres, who was born and grew up in El Barrio and has been a criminal lawyer, an assistant district attorney for New York County, a county criminal court judge and, since 1979, a judge in the state supreme court. Two of his novels, *Carlito's Way* and *After Hours*, are about Carlito Brigante, a hood with a strong upward mobility drive, and about the world Carlito has emerged from:

> *Who are these people? Puerto Ricans. They come from an island a hundred long by thirty-five miles wide. They come in all sizes, colors and shapes. They got a little of everybody. Heart like the Jews, soul like the Blacks, balls like the Italians. They hit New York in the 1940s, the wrong time. But like when is it right, when your face don't help, your accent ain't French, and your clothes don't fit? They hung in anyway—most of the tickets were one way. So they filed into the roach stables in Harlem and the South Bronx. They sat behind the sewing machines and stood behind the steam tables. In other words, they busted their ass, they went for the Dream, most of them.*[19]

What these books are about is Carlito's quest for the Dream through the avenues of organized crime, still controlled by what remains of the old Mafia empire but increasingly open to penetration by enterprising blacks and Puerto Ricans. They belong to the genre of the underworld novel as much as they do to Nuyorican literature and have closer affinities with the work of George Higgins than with that of Piri Thomas. The success Torres has achieved in the field of law is mirrored in Carlito's upside-down world of crime. Both are walking, along different streets, toward the Dream. Both have left El Barrio and entered the mainstream, Carlito as hood, Torres and writer and judge.

NOTES

1. Miguel Piñero, *Short Eyes*, p. 30
2. Ibid., p. 37.
3. Ibid., p. 40.
4. Ibid., p. 115.

5. Ibid., p. 117.
6. Ibid., p. 118.
7. Ibid., p. 119.
8. Miguel Piñero, *The Sun Always Shines for the Cool*, p. 181.
9. Ibid., p. 193.
10. Ibid., p. 202.
11. Ibid., p. 194.
12. Miguel Algarín and Miguel Piñero, eds., *Nuyorican Poetry*, p. 26.
13. Piñero, *The Sun Always Shines*, pp. 199-200.
14. Ibid., p. 201.
15. Ibid., p. 185.
16. Jaime Carrero, *Raquelo tiene un mensaje*, p. 133.
17. Ibid., p. 154.
18. Ester Comas, *Hello Stranger*, p. 15.
19. Edwin Torres, *Carlito's Way*, p. 3.

AFTERWORD

There are no minority rights programs in literary criticism: the
literature of New York's Puerto Rican population is subject to
the same types of judgments as any other body of writing, judgments based on human insight and on formal control and originality. When these norms of content and style are applied to the
books discussed above, some idea can be projected of their merit
in terms of broader literary contexts.

Puerto Rican ethnic writing is the most complete description
we have of the process of immigration that is so conspicuous a
part of American history. Its most valuable literary component is
the insight offered into the cultural and psychological reactions
of individuals passing through this critical, often painful experience. It is tempting to imagine that the United States, a nation of
immigrants, would be an easy place to which to migrate, but the
evidence shows that this is not the case for several reasons.
First, the migratory experience is inherently difficult. The adult
migrant, especially the poor and uneducated migrant who has
few resources beyond the confines of his native culture, is faced
with the immense task of learning a new set of life responses at
an age when learning no longer comes easily. Problems of practical living are involved, but also problems of self-identification
aggravated by language, by the image projected upon one by
other segments of the new society, and by the need to reconcile
old and new standards of feeling and conduct. The "successful"
immigrant in American mythology is one who, like Pedro Labarthe
and Richard Ruiz, adapts to the new system and makes it work

in his favor. This type of adaptation is not common. More typical is the pattern discussed in Chapter 2—the attempt by people who leave their homes primarily in hope of economic betterment to transplant the life of the old country into the body of the new. This results in the creation of a ghetto, which fosters emotional security but retards assimilation. Since most immigrants are poor, poverty thickens in the ghetto and prepares the way for sickness, misery, and crime.

The children of immigrants—either born on the mainland or brought there at an early age—pass through a terrible conflict between the parental image and the new language, popular culture, and institutions with which the children want desperately to identify. This conflict and their confusion over larger social relationships lead them, during adolescence, to membership in street gangs, ad hoc societies that satisfy the need for belonging and for understandable social order and prepare their members to establish some sort of relationship to mainstream society as they grow to adulthood.

This relationship, largely predetermined for the first generation, varies widely in the second. Successful assimilation is seen in the judicial career of Edwin Torres and in his character Carlito's progress in the Mafia. The characters in Nicholasa Mohr's books show increasing adaptation to mainstream norms while demanding accommodation for parental habits and values. But other authors reveal serious problems. Jesus Colon, Piri Thomas, and Manuel Manrique reveal how, within the powerful racial substructure of American society, newcomers with African features can assimilate only by identifying with the black minority, which is also ghetto-locked but which has an established niche in the national ecology. It is at this point that El Barrio ceases to be simply an immigrant enclave and becomes instead part of that increasingly fixed and homogeneous subculture known as the inner city. It is here, too, that Nuyorican writing joins with black literature specifically in exploring a contemporary urban microworld in which poverty, exploitation, social despair, drugs, crime, rats, and roaches are distinctive elements in the communal experience.

From the recognition and acceptance of this experience—the only experience on which countless human lives are nourished—there emerges in the mature Piri Thomas, in Nicholasa Mohr's

In Nueva York, and in poets like Pedro Pietri and Miguel Piñero the concept that the apparent failure and disorder of the inner city contain elements that can be reshaped into a new and satisfying lifestyle, an alternative, for those who live it, to the mainstream *weltanshauung*, which has, until recently, shown little tolerance for competition. This challenge to the traditional Establishment of conduct and values leads, finally, to Miguel Algarín's defense of a local third world, a variety of different societies, each with its own goals and behavior patterns and ideals, operating within the framework of a truly pluralistic nation. Some of these societies may be ethnic in origin, but they borrow from one another and from popular culture, and their inspiration is a native response to native conditions. They have parallels, moreover, among the Amish and other groups which have managed to maintain their distinctive ethos within the American social and political systems.

It should be understood that this diachronic reconstruction of the immigration process leads to no easy generalizations about the present composition of New York's Puerto Rican community, which contains individuals at each stage of the process. The migration is always starting over. Common citizenship and geographic proximity, moreover, make possible continuous two-way population exchanges between the Island and the mainland, so at any given moment the city houses unrecorded numbers of Puerto Ricans who are there temporarily to spend time with relatives, to be on hand for fluctuating employment opportunities, or even to use the city's superior social services. These transient residents, largely overlooked in both literary and sociological writing, confuse the public and professional picture of the true immigrants. It is sometimes asked, for example, why a community that has been in the country for so long has had so little success learning English and improving itself economically. One answer is that the most successful members of the community merge into other communities and are replaced by new arrivals and temporary residents who have no intention of establishing themselves permanently in the Promised Land. Another answer is the small but persistent sentiment favoring Puerto Rican independence, which provides a face-saving rationale for failure to "make it" in Gringolandia.

The picture is further complicated by illegal aliens from Latin American and the Hispanic Caribbean who, sometimes equipped with false birth or baptismal certificates, blend irretrievably into the Puerto Rican population, a development first pointed out by Bernardo Vega. Little is known about these uninvited guests; their whole endeavor is to remain officially invisible. But except for the Cubans, who come from a monied class, the experience of most Central and South American immigrants is likely to resemble that of the Puerto Ricans who preceded them. One of the nonliterary contributions of Nuyorican literature is its potential usefulness in predicting the pattern of future Hispanic immigration.

The formal literary attainments of this body of writing vary considerably. At one extreme, the memoirs of Bernardo Vega, Pedro Juan Labarthe, and Richard Ruiz, like the autobiography of Benjamin Franklin, are straightforward records with no pretention of original style or organization. Their merit as personal and social documents lies partly in their literary innocence. At the other extreme, the short stories of Nicholasa Mohr, the novels of Edwin Torres, and the novels, stories, and plays of Jaime Carrero and the Puerto Rican authors discussed in Chapter 2 show a high degree of proficiency in the use of established genres and literary techniques.

The most characteristic Nuyorican writers, however, are those of limited formal education who have attempted to fashion their own language resources into vehicles suitable for expressing an experience without exact counterpart and a personal interpretation of that experience. Among prose writers Piri Thomas remains the most noteworthy of these experimenters. His contrived yet plausible combination of slang, ghetto rhetoric, Spanish borrowings, and energetic speech rhythms constitutes a unique style that, while not flexible enough for the import of his maturer work, is an excellent carrier of his personality and formative influences. The Barrio writers who followed and sometimes imitated Thomas have not added substantially to his achievement.

Thomas's true heirs in the creation of a native literary idiom for Nuyoricans are the young poets who have come to accept, without apology, membership in a black-Puerto Rican-inner city culture, which they see as a valid alternative to the traditional patterns of americanization. To Thomas's innovations they have added irony, elements from popular mainstream culture, and greater esthetic sophistication and self-awareness. Within a common poetic they have managed enough flexibility to produce styles as distinctive as those of Pedro Pietri, Tato Laviera, Miguel Algarín, and Miguel Piñero. In their work what began and developed as immigrant writing claims its American birthright and takes its place within an increasingly pluralistic national literature.

What will become of specifically Nuyorican literature? As a body of writing identified by a common immigration experience or by common ethnic and cultural roots it will probably disappear. Even if the immigration continues, and it will, books continuing to dwell upon it would inevitably become repetitious and convention-ridden. Ethnic identification is already weakening in second-generation writers. Piñero's published plays, for example, have almost no references to Puerto Rico or its traditions; his characters—Anglos, blacks, Puerto Ricans—share a minority status open to all persons without regard to race, religion, or national origin. If past developments are any clue to the future, Puerto Rican immigrant writing will follow the Puerto Ricans themselves into the mainstream. In only one important subgenre, the Jewish-American novel, has an ethnic label survived the immigrant literature which preceded it. Eugene O'Neill and John Ciardi are as American as apple pie: so, in their inner-city ways, are Piri Thomas, Nicholasa Mohr, and Miky Piñero.

BIBLIOGRAPHY

Abramson, Michael, and The Young Lords Party. *Palante: Young Lords Party.* New York: McGraw-Hill, 1971.

Acosta-Belén, Edna. "Conversations with Nicholasa Mohr." *Revista Chicano-Riqueña* 8, no. 2 (1980): 35-41.

Agostini de del Río, Amelia. *Puertorriqueños en Nueva York.* New York: Editorial Mensaje, 1970.

Algarín, Miguel. *Mongo Affair.* New York: Nuyorican Poet's Café, Inc., 1978.

————. *On Call.* Houston Tex.: Arte Público Press, 1980.

————, and Miguel Piñero, eds. *Nuyorican Poetry.* New York: William Morrow, 1975).

Ashton, Guy T. "The Return and Re-Return of Long-Term Puerto Rican Migrants: A Selective Rural-Urban Sample." *Revista/Review Interamericana* 10, no. 1 (1980): 27-45.

Barradas, Efraín, and Rafael Rodríguez, eds. *Herejes y mitificadores: Muestra de poesía puertorriqueña en los Estados Unidos.* San Juan: Ediciones Huracán, 1980).

Barreto, Lefty. *Nobody's Hero.* New York: New American Library, 1976.

Benítez, Jaime. "El problema humano de la emigración." *La Torre* 4, no. 13 (1956): 13-31.

Carrero, Jaime. *Jet Neorriqueño: Neo-Rican Jetliner.* San Germán, P.R.: Universidad Interamericana, 1964.

————. *Raquelo tiene un mensaje.* San Juan, privately printed, 1970.

————. *Pipo Subway no sabe reir.* In *Teatro.* Río Piedras, P.R.: Ediciones Puerto, 1973, pp. 113-57.

————. *The FM Safe. Revista Chicano-Riqueña* 7, no.1 (1979): 110-50.

Cayo Sexton, Patricia. *Spanish Harlem: Anatomy of Poverty.* New York: Harper & Row, 1965.

Chenault, Lawrence R. *The Puerto Rican Migrant in New York City.* New York: Columbia University Press, 1938.

Cintrón, Humberto. *Frankie Cristo.* New York: Taino Publishing Co., 1972.

Colon, Jesus. *A Puerto Rican in New York and Other Sketches.* New York: Mainstream Publisher, 1961.

Colon, Ramon. *Carlos Tapia: A Puerto Rican Hero in New York.* New York: Vantage Press, 1976.

Comas, Ester. *Hello Stranger.* New York: n.p., 1971

Cordasco, Francesco; Eugene Bucchioni; and Diego Castellanos. *Puerto Ricans on the United States Mainland: A Bibliography of Reports, Texts, Critical Studies and Related Materials.* Totowa, N.J.: Rowman & Littlefield, 1972.

Cotto-Thorner, Guillermo. *Trópico en Manhattan.* San Juan: Editorial Cordillera, 1967.

Cruz, Nicky. *Run Baby Run.* Plainfield, N.J.: Logos Books, 1968.

Díaz Soler, Luis M. "Relaciones raciales en Puerto Rico." *Revista/Review Interamericana* 3, no. 1 (1973): 61-72.

Díaz Valcárcel, Emilio. *Harlem todos los días.* San Juan: Ediciones Huracán, 1978.

Fernández Méndez, Eugenio. "¿Asimilación o enquistamiento?" *La Torre* 4, no. 13 (1956): 137-46.

Figueroa, José Angel. *East 110th Street.* Detroit, Mich.: Broadside Press, 1973.

Fishman, Joshua A.; Robert L. Cooper; and Roxana Ma, eds. *Bilingualism in the Barrio.* New York: U.S. Department of Health, Education, and Welfare, 1968.

Fitzpatrick, Joseph P. *Puerto Rican Americans: The Meaning of Migration to the Mainland.* Englewood Cliffs, N.J.: Prentice-Hall, 1971.

Flores, Juan. "Back Down These Mean Streets: Introducing Nicholasa Mohr and Louis Reyes Rivera." *Revista Chicano-Riqueña* 8, no. 2 (1980): 51-56.

Handlin, Oscar. *The Newcomers: Negroes and Puerto Ricans in a Changing Metropolis.* Cambridge, Mass.: Harvard Univ. Press, 1959.

Hernandez, Pedro L. *There Is No Tomorrow.* New York: Vantage Press, 1978.

Hernandez Cruz, Victor. *Snaps.* New York: Vintage-Random House, 1969.

———. *Mainland.* New York: Random House, 1973.

Iglesias, César Andreu, ed. *Memorias de Bernardo Vega: Una contribución a la historia de la comunidad puertorriqueña en Nueva York.* San Juan: Ediciones Huracán, 1977.

International Migration Review 13, no. 2 (1979).

Klau, Susan L. "The Use of Spanish and the Works of Piri Thomas." Ph.D. dissertation, University of Puerto Rico, 1977.

Labarthe, Pedro Juan. *The Son of Two Nations: The Private Life of a Columbia Student.* New York: Carranza & Co., 1931.

Laguerre, Enrique A. *La ceiba en el tiesto.* San Juan: Biblioteca de Autores Puertorriqueños, 1956.

———. *El fuego y su aire.* Buenos Aires: Editorial Losada, 1970.

Laviera, Tato. *La Carreta Made a U-Turn.* 2nd ed. Houston, Tex.: Arte Público Press, 1981.

Levine, Barry B. *Benjy López: A Picaresque Tale of Emigration and Return.* New York: Basic Books, 1979.

Lewis, Oscar. *La Vida: A Puerto Rican Family in the Culture of Poverty—San Juan and New York.* New York: Random House, 1965.

López, Adalberto. "Literature for the Puerto Rican Diaspora." *Caribbean Review* 5, no. 2 (1973): 5-11.

———. "Literature for the Puerto Rican Diaspora: Part II." *Caribbean Review* 6, no. 4 (1974): 41-46.

Manrique Manuel. *Island in Harlem.* New York: John Day, 1966.

Mapp, Edward, ed. *Puerto Rican Perspectives.* Metuchen, N.J.: Scarecrow Press, 1974.

Marqués, René. *La carreta.* In *Teatro puertorriqueño: Cuarto festival.* San Juan: Instituto de Cultura Puertorriqueña, 1962, pp. 317-563. (Trans. Charles Pilditch. *The Oxcart.* New York: Scribner's, 1969.)

Matilla, Alfredo, and Iván Silén, eds. *The Puerto Rican Poets/Los Poetas Puertorriqueños.* New York: Bantam, 1972.

Meléndez, Jesús Papoleto. *Street Poetry and Other Poems.* New York: Barlenmir House, 1972.

Méndez Ballester, Manuel. *Encrucijada.* In *Teatro puertorriqueño: Primer festival.* San Juan: Instituto de Cultura Puertorriqueña, 1959, pp. 19-172.

Miller, John C. "Nicholasa Mohr: Neorican Writing in Progress: 'A View of the Other Culture.'" *Revista/Review Interamericana* 9, no. 4 (1979/80): 543-49.

Mills, C. Wright; Clarence Senior; and Rose Kohn Goldsen. *The Puerto Rican Journey: New York's Newest Migrants.* New York: Harper & Row, 1950.

Mohr, Eugene V. "Fifty Years of Puerto Rican Literature in English—1923-1973: An Annotated Bibliography." *Revista/Review Interamericana* 3, no. 3 (1973): 290-98.

Mohr, Nicholasa. *Nilda.* 1973; rpt. ed. New York: Bantam, 1974.

———. *El Bronx Remembered.* 1975; rpt. New York: Bantam, 1976.

————. *In Nueva York.* New York: Dell, 1977.

————. *Felita.* New York: The Dial Press, 1979.

Morse, Dean W. *Pride Against Prejudice: Work in the Lives of Older Blacks and Young Puerto Ricans.* Conservation of Human Resources Series, 9. Montclair, N.J.: Allanheld Osmun, 1980.

Padilla, Elena. *Up From Puerto Rico.* New York: Columbia Univ. Press, 1958.

Pietri, Pedro. *Puerto Rican Obituary.* New York: Monthly Review Press, 1973.

Piñero, Miguel. *Short Eyes.* New York: Hill and Wang, 1975.

————. *The Sun Always Shines for the Cool. Revista Chicano-Riqueña* 7, no. 1 (1979): 173-204.

————. *La Bodega Sold Dreams.* Houston, Tex.: Arte Público Press, 1980.

Puertorriqueños en los Estados Unidos Continentales: Un futuro incierto. Washington, D.C.: Comisión de Derechos Civiles de los Estados Unidos, 1976.

Rand, Christopher. *The Puerto Ricans.* New York: Oxford University Press, 1958.

Ramírez de Arellano, Diana. *La cultura en el panorama puertorriqueño de Nueva York.* New York: n.p., 1964.

Rivera, Edward. "La Situación." *New York,* 7 August 1972, pp. 51-55.

————. "A Little Lavabo." *The Bilingual Review/La Revista Bilingue* 2, nos. 1 and 2 (1975): 184-91.

Robles, Rafaela R.; Ruth Martínez; and Margarita Moscoso. *Puerto Rican Return Migration: Impact on the Migrant and the Island.* San Juan: University of Puerto Rico School of Public Health, 1980.

Ruiz, Richard. *The Hungry American.* Bend, Ore.: Maverick Publications, 1978.

Sánchez Korrol, Virginia. "On the Other Side of the Ocean: The Work Experiences of Early Puerto Rican Migrant Women." *Caribbean Review* 8, no. 1 (1979): 22-28.

Seda Bonilla, Eduardo. "On the Vicissitudes of Being 'Puerto Rican': An Exploration of Pedro Juan Soto's *Hot Land, Cold Season.*" *Revista/Review Interamericana* 8, no. 1 (1978): 116-28.

Senior, Clarence. *The Puerto Ricans: Strangers—Then Neighbors.* Chicago: Quadrangle Books, 1965.

Sheehan, Susan. *A Welfare Mother.* Boston: Houghton Mifflin, 1976.

Soto, Pedro Juan. *Spiks.* Mexico: Los Presentes, 1956. (Trans. Victoria Ortiz. *Spiks.* New York: Monthly Review Press, 1973.)

————. *Ardiente suelo, fría estación.* Xalapa, Mexico: Universidad Veracruzana, 1961. (Trans. Helen R. Lane. *Hot Land, Cold Season.* New York: Dell, 1971.)

Thomas, Piri. *Down These Mean Streets.* 1967; rpt. ed. New York: New American Library, 1968.

———. *Savior, Savior, Hold My Hand.* New York: Doubleday, 1972.

———. *Seven Long Times.* New York: Praeger, 1974.

———. *Stories from El Barrio.* New York: Knopf, 1978.

Torres, Edwin. *Carlito's Way.* New York: Saturday Review Press, 1975.

———. *After Hours.* New York: Dial Press, 1979.

Vega, Bernardo. *See* Iglesias, César Andreu, ed.

Vivas Maldonado, J. L. *A vellón las esperanzas, o Melania.* New York: Las Americas, 1971.

Vivó, Paquita. *The Puerto Ricans: An Annotated Bibliography.* New York: R. R. Bowker, 1973.

Wagenheim, Kal. *Survey of Puerto Ricans on the U.S. Mainland in the 1970s.* New York: Praeger, 1975.

Wakefield, Dan. *Island in the City: The World of Spanish Harlem.* Boston: Houghton Mifflin, 1959.

INDEX

About the Author

EUGENE V. MOHR is Professor of English at the University of Puerto Rico. He has written *The Other Caribbean: Concerns of West Indian Writing* and *Examining the English Exam: A Study of the Linguistic Content of ESLAT,* as well as articles on language, Caribbean literature, and the teaching of English.